Praise for
"Jehovah has Healed"

I am so honored and grateful to read this faith-boosting book. Dr. Carine Njoh is one of the spiritual women I look up to, and I can categorically tell you that she is a strong woman; a woman of crazy faith by the grace of God. The saying "One day you'll tell your story of how you've overcome what you're going through now, and it will become part of someone else's survival guide", summarizes it all. Yes! This is the survival guide that points you back to God and His word, that He is your anchor, hope and the only source of survival in stormy seasons.

Do you have any unanswered questions in your mind, or do you have the wrong perspective about who God is, because of the challenges that life is throwing at you? Do you experience constant disappointment at every edge of breakthrough? This is the book for you. It will teach you how to respond positively to negative situations; how to hold on to God's promises and know beyond every shadow of doubt that God will always come through, even when everything seems hopeless.

This is a testament that God is still in the business of turning every negative situation around for your good when you "stick" with Him. Lamentations 3:25(NLT) "The Lord is good to those who depend on Him, to those who search for Him". Total dependence on God pays!

Without any iota of exaggeration, I was in awe while reading this and my faith has been greatly strengthened with this amazing testimony. I am excited for what God will do in your lives through this book. Please be open as you read this because the Holy Spirit will have His way in you only to the extent at which you open up to Him. I pray that as you read this book, you'll have an encounter with the love of the Father and the insatiable hunger for Him will be stirred in you. Be blessed.

-Mary Omoyele

The words of this Woman of God in writing through these pages are an encouragement to every soul out there. People have gone through stuff which they think can't be uttered until they read a book such as this. This is a typical example of the fact that all the Glory will be given to God always. Just like the book alludes, in the end, we always win.

I am so touched by the words in this book and I know it is meant to change lives and destinies. God has not forgotten your situation. You would never be able to tell Carine has gone through what she wrote, because she maintained an attitude of gratitude all along this journey, she chose to embrace it and it has paid off and will continue to do so for His Glory as she rightly mentioned.

"I can't erase my story, but I choose to tell it, because I use it for His Glory".

-Sister Atsi

Dearly beloved, you are in for an encounter. If you are facing any challenges, and you are not sure where the puzzle comes together in your life, this book is definitely a must read. Carine Njoh opens up, speaking from experience, and walks us through her process of healing ; trusting God and also the process He takes her through. The Holy Ghost will minister to you and open things up to you even as you read through the pages of this book. Read with an open mind and be expectant. You will be blessed.

-Anita Odartey-Addo

This book was hard for me to put down as I experienced all the pictures of her challenges and God's faithfulness came back so fresh in my mind as I read. There are many Christian Books out there but there are not many that deal with the challenges mother's go through and how God shows up for them. This book is greatly influenced by the Holy Spirit to bring healing and show others God's faithfulness. I strongly believe that God wants to use this book to comfort and heal many people in the world. This book is a mother's journey that has been reserved for our generation to move us to a new level in our walk with God in spite of our challenges. Living in the end times, this book will help us to go beyond what science/doctors say about our conditions and learn to trust God.

I had the privilege to watch Dr. Mrs. Carine Njoh develop and grow in her walk with the Lord. I saw some of her encounters in the presence of God and watched how God used her to minister to others through healing, word of knowledge and the use of different languages which by herself she couldn't speak nor understand. What drew me close to her was her love for God and her humility. I observed her humility, commitment, integrity, passion for God, her deep hunger to know God more and how she served others in her own special way. For many years now, I have learned a lot from her while spending time with her at church, praying with her at her home and attending conferences with her. She is completely sold out for Christ Jesus.

Watching her go through so much loss, her level of faith and stability through her journey of motherhood is mind blowing. It is easy for people to say they love the

Lord Jesus when things are working, but the true love of Jesus is seen when you go through challenges and you choose to stand and testify of His goodness. Dr. Carine is a good example of a woman who loves the Lord and has authority to speak and minister comfort and healing to others because she has walked through the process. Her journey is a good example of King David's expression in Psalm 23:4 when he was going through challenges.

In this book she makes us understand that challenges are not from God but through the process, God is always with us and we should learn to trust the situation He is taking us through because God is always faithful. Jesse and Josiah are the evidence of God's faithfulness. Our challenges do not define us but our actions do, how we react to challenges determines our tomorrow. We don't have to accept what life gives us; we have to draw from life what we want based on God's promises to us. Critical challenges in life produce miraculous results when we depend on God as Dr Carine did.

I wish to encourage you to open your heart for God to give you encounters as you read this book. You might not be going through the same challenges Dr. Carine went through, but know that the same God that helped her will also help you when you call on Him as seen in Psalm 107:19-20. Your present state/challenge is not your final state because God will clothe you with gladness (Psalms 30: 11). Don't be discouraged about what you are going through, for every champion has a painful story. You have to make up your mind to walk by faith and not by sight (2 Corinthians 5:7) in order to have victory over challenges.

I highly recommend this book to everybody as a must-read.

-Hilda Njenne Ageh (Pastor Glory)

This book is a must read for everyone. It is an absolute necessity for those who have gone through inexplicable, life altering, gut-wrenching circumstances. Dr. Njoh's life story is proof that even though we cannot explain certain things and we do not understand many things, God is always at work. God is at work bringing good out of evil, joy out of sorrow and life out of death! If you want to understand how to wait on God, grow in Christ, submit and love Him despite your circumstances, read this book. This testimony is proof that God truly gives his children "beauty for ashes" and "a garment of praise for the garment of mourning." May I suggest you please grab a box of tissue as you read because it's a tearjerker.

-Ethel G. Nkwanyuo
The Eat Less Pray More Movement.

I have never read any book this heart touching. It is no doubt that this book was written by the inspiration of the Holy Spirit. The author is very private and for her to write about the story of her life is something to take seriously. Everybody needs a boost in their faith sometimes. This book is a must have for everyone going through challenging situations, especially mothers in waiting. God will surely come through for you. Dr Carine Njoh is a woman of faith. My trust and total dependence in God was stirred up at her daughter's funeral, when she encouraged everyone that was present to have faith in God. I have never seen something like that.

Job 13:15 says "Though He slay me, yet will I trust in Him". Dr Carine Njoh is a lover of God. She has bulldog faith and she is a role model to every young woman. She is on fire for God. Despite everything she went through, her fire for God increased. Being part of her cell group meeting and a prayer group she organized monthly, called Upper Room, my life has changed tremendously. The Bible says seek the Lord while He may be found, call on Him while He is near. The time to seek God is now. God has better plans for us all. This book really touched my soul. Your testimony is closer than you think. Stay focused. Stay strong.

-Isambi Tuma

"Jehovah Has Healed" is a perfect read to get a great insight about true love, peace, joy, hope, resilience, stamina, and steadfastness. The manner in which she and her husband took care of their ailing children and her relentless desire to know God intimately portrays true love and steadfastness. This book portrays a sister who is always joyful and never portrays any inch of stress in her life. The benefit of always celebrating with others whether during weddings, pregnancies, births and baby dedications is emphasized in this book. This book will encourage you to never give up your heart's desire till all comes to pass indicating a resilient and determined spirit. In reading this book, one can get great inspiration from a woman who has trusted, dedicated and believed God throughout all the storms she encountered in her life and came out triumphantly. If you truly want to be encouraged to look past your challenges in life, please read this book and share with others who might be blessed which is the sole purpose of writing this book.

-Dr. Geraldine Sellu

I first met Carine and Victor when they brought Jesse to the church class I taught when he was 2 or 3 years old. I witnessed this young couple go through a most difficult time but they continued to bring Jesse to church. It was obvious their faith was very, very strong and kept them going.

During visits with Victor and Carine over the years, I sometimes sensed their pain but they were always quick to praise God and cling to His Word.

In "Jehovah Has Healed", Carine pours out her heart and fills in the gaps with details that she mostly kept to herself. I feel it is her hope and prayer that by sharing her story she might help others who are struggling with tragic and difficult times, that they might draw their strength from God as she has.

God has sure kept His hand on Victor & Carine.

-Brenda Hager

My dear friend and co-laborer in the kingdom has, with this lovely book of her personal journey of faith, hope and love, opened up to us a place to encounter inner healing, restoration and the overwhelming power of God.

I recommend this book to every believer going through their process as this will encourage and strengthen them from the inner man as it did to me.

-Christy Ayoo

Thank God for giving Carine the grace, inspiration, courage and time to put these facts of her life together. This work is a masterpiece and not just another book. Carine shares a coherent and captivating story line. Going through each chapter is like watching a movie, thereby arousing the interest and curiosity of the reader to know what follows. Blessed be the name of the Lord for giving you such a wonderful husband, who has been and will be there for you.

I am convinced that as people read through this book, it will change their way of thinking, their view and perception of life vis-à-vis God and above all shape and reshape lives.

-Martha Kombe Monono
President & Founder, First Ladies International Network

Jehovah
has
Healed

A MOTHER'S JOURNEY
THROUGH LOSS, FAITH, AND THE
SUPERNATURAL

Dr. CARINE NDEH NJOH

DEDICATION

This book is dedicated to Nasia and Eliana.

Thank you for allowing me to mother you two. In caring for you, you taught me strength and resilience. Because of you, I was able to search for the deeper things of God, which led to my passionate pursuit of Him. For that, I am eternally grateful.

ACKNOWLEDGMENTS

My deepest appreciation…

My dear husband Victor: You're the behind-the-scenes powerhouse. Thank you for being a strong pillar throughout this process. I don't know of anyone who would have been a better partner to walk through this journey with. Thank you for understanding me. Thank you for putting up with my different emotions and allowing me to pursue my passion.

My parents: Thank you for raising me in a godly home and for teaching me all the valuable lessons to navigate this life.

My siblings: Kenneth, Jane, Laura, Yvonne and Joyce, thank you for always standing by me and accepting me just as I am, even when you didn't understand me. You all have been a solid pillar and this process made our bond closer than ever.

My children: Jesse and Josiah, thank you for being the wonderful kids you are and cooperating with me throughout the process of writing this book.

Stacy Shaneyfelt: Thank you for your skill and attention to detail in the initial editing of the manuscript.

My Pastor: Thank you so much for pushing me out of my comfort zone. I am grateful for all the lessons you have taught me through the years.

My Church family: You are a wonderful support system! Thank you for all the love.

My village of friends and extended family: Thank you for standing with me even when you didn't have to. I appreciate you all.

Abba Father: Lord, I say thank You for holding my hand through it all. Without You, I do not know where I would be. Thank You for being faithful even when I wasn't. Thank You for laying it on my heart to put this experience on paper, and for giving me the grace to write it, even through the most difficult parts.

FOREWORD

Dr. Carine has given the body of Christ a great treasure in this work. It is not only inspiring, but faith lifting, engaging, captivating and reasonably balanced. She has tried to successfully address the very contentious subject of how Christians tackle their moments of tragedy.

Her narrative of these events points her out as a woman set apart for great things.

The whole account in this book is about Satan's spirited attempts to scuttle and weaken the faith of a major 'voice' in these end times. This work is a reminder that being a believer does not automatically exempt one from the fiery darts of the enemy. She has been wonderfully open about her vulnerabilities as a human being during the years she walked through this 'fire'. She is genuine enough to admit that there were moments she had questions, and questioned, along the way. Not many believers would dare to admit this openly, though they privately struggle with such feelings. Sister Carine, thank you for reminding us that the anointed also cry!

In this book, she vividly demonstrates the power of faith in God, regardless of the pressures that were ever present, to bring about outstanding miracles in the face of grave impossibilities.

The whole experience gave her the opportunity to look at life deeply. Through this experience, she has emerged a stronger, deeper and more philosophical person; what the enemy meant for evil, God has certainly turned around for good.

As her pastor for many years, I can confidently say that her life, and that of her family members, is a testament to the truth that all power belongs to God. In the words of the Jesus Culture song:

"Love has a Name, Victory has a Name, Joy has a Name, and that Name is Jesus."

Through Carine's process, she stayed true and was able to demonstrate that.

Jesus is Lord!

-Pastor Joshua Aghasedo

Resident Pastor Christ Apostolic Church,
WOSEM aka Miracle City
Oklahoma City, OK

PREFACE

Over the last 10 years, I have been through some very difficult times. It seemed like waking up from one nightmare, seeing the nightmare before me, going back to sleep and waking up from another nightmare. I knew my only hope was God. I decided to totally depend on Him. Through each trial, I saw the Lord hold my hand. He gave me the grace to live through and overcome every trial.

In 2017, He instructed me to begin writing about the journey He was taking me through. I started writing the story as He brought to my memory very vivid incidents. Being a private person by nature, there were some things I did not want to share with the world. A few times, I'd type and then delete, and I heard Him gently tell me to put everything back in writing. I paused sometime in 2018, because I knew the book wasn't complete. I knew some events would have to unfold for the book to be complete, but I didn't know how that was going to happen. I just had to put my trust in God, and believe that He is too faithful to fail. Fast forward to 2020, everything came full circle and I'm now able to share my story for the glory of God. In the face of challenges, if we stick with the Word of God, and the God of the Word, He will come through for us.

LIFE IS EASY,
WHEN YOU'RE UP ON THE MOUNTAIN

AND YOU'VE GOT PEACE OF MIND,
LIKE YOU'VE NEVER KNOWN

BUT THINGS CHANGE,
WHEN YOU'RE DOWN IN THE VALLEY

DON'T LOSE FAITH,
FOR YOU'RE NEVER ALONE

FOR THE GOD ON THE MOUNTAIN,
IS STILL GOD IN THE VALLEY

WHEN THINGS GO WRONG,
HE'LL MAKE THEM RIGHT

AND THE GOD OF THE GOOD TIMES,
IS STILL GOD IN THE BAD TIMES

THE GOD OF THE DAY,
IS STILL GOD IN THE NIGHT

YOU TALK OF FAITH,
WHEN YOU'RE UP ON THE MOUNTAIN

BUT TALK COMES SO EASY,
WHEN LIFE'S AT IT'S BEST

NOW IT'S DOWN IN THE VALLEYS,
OF TRIALS AND TEMPTATIONS

THAT'S WHERE YOUR FAITH,
IS REALLY PUT TO THE TEST

FOR THE GOD ON THE MOUNTAIN,
IS STILL GOD IN THE VALLEY

WHEN THINGS GO WRONG,
HE'LL MAKE THEM RIGHT

AND THE GOD OF THE GOOD TIMES,
IS STILL GOD IN THE BAD TIMES

THE GOD OF THE DAY,
IS STILL GOD IN THE NIGHT

THE GOD OF THE DAY,
IS STILL GOD IN THE NIGHT

Bill & Gloria Gaither

TABLE OF CONTENTS

INTRODUCTION

Two decades of congregational care in three continents have given me the honor to serve families and individuals in their most vulnerable place of experiencing death and grieving the loss of a loved one. The privilege to be allowed into their inner circle of mourning and walking through the healing process over the following months and years are invaluable. Yet the global pandemic of 2020 has produced a global avalanche of death and grief that has marked our generation in ways that it might take decades to come close to healing from. It is with this backdrop that I introduce "Jehovah has Healed" a captivating and compelling memoir of hope, loss, pain, and the triumph of faith.

The Irish apologist C. S. Lewis, in "The Problem of Pain" (p. 92) said ".... we will admit that we can ignore even pleasure. But pain insists upon being attended to. God whispers to us in our pleasures, speaks in our conscience, but shouts in our pain". The providence of God during life's most challenging situations is that He is right there in our pain and always available if we will call. Carine has always been admired for her depth of compassion and authenticity. The integrity and dependability by which she is defined by her closest family and friends makes her a deeply loved person.

The level of vulnerability she provides her reader is amazing, especially, for the culture she grew up in. She grapples with the joys and tragedies of motherhood with significant candor. She shares with us, the uniquely private pains and trauma of miscarriages filled with its own anxieties and fears, yet the overarching strength of her story of redemption is one of trust in the Heavenly Father's goodness and unfailing love.

As the sweet Psalmist and King of Israel puts it in the Holy Scriptures, "I would have despaired had I not believed that I would see the goodness of the Lord in the land of the living." Psalm 27:13.

"Jehovah Has Healed" will empower you and inspire you to grieve in a healthier way. It will challenge you to be honest with yourself and in your relationships with others, without ever losing the compassion and kindness that is a hallmark of great friendship. It will inspire you to cultivate a lifestyle that is less selfish, self-centered, and self-absorbed as you learn to give more of yourself away. Her story consistently underscores the importance of cultivating community. To live life with people of shared values especially one with faith in the Creator at its center.

The healing process of grief really can be varied and different for every human being in every culture on earth. However, without a doubt the value of staying thankful, positive, and having strong family ties go a long way in the journey of recovery. A journey that strengthens us, as we learn to trust the process. Carine's personal story qualifies her to speak to a deep part of you in an incredibly unique manner that few can or will. If you permit it, it really might be her heavenly Father reaching out to shape your heart and life in a way only He can as Creator.

-Pastor Charles Ikutiminu
Founder, Cross Passion Ministries International

Chapter 1
Marvels of Motherhood

"No occupation in this world is more trying to soul and body than the care of young children. What patience and wisdom, skill and unlimited love it calls for. God gave the work to mothers and furnished them for it, and they cannot shirk it and be guiltless.

-Isabella Alden

My journey literally began in West Africa. I was born in the mountainous city of Buea, Cameroon, and studied in Cameroon until high school where I passed my Advanced Levels. I visited the United States in the late 90s, sometimes during the winter breaks, but mostly summer holidays. I finally moved to America in May of 2001, where I started college in the little college town of Weatherford, OK. Like most African parents, when you go abroad, they expect you to pursue the degree you initially targeted, so they could eventually come to celebrate upon your graduation.

Almost every woman has a dream of getting married to the right man and building a beautiful family together. My own dreams weren't any different. I always dreamed of the man I was going to marry and the family we were going to raise together. In college, I met my husband,

Victor, and we started dating around 2002. He proposed to me five years into our relationship; however, when I informed my dad, we had to keep it on the down low. Dad insisted I couldn't get married until I finished school and reminded me how in our culture, 'Your first husband is your book.' In turn, I followed his advice and continued school.

Several years later, once I was almost done with my professional program, my husband's family had contacted my dad and our traditional marriage was conducted at home . A few months later, we decided to do the Court signing here in the U.S, since I only had a year left before graduating college. We had family and friends come together and we signed our court wedding on May 16th 2008. Most African parents always dream of their kids going back home to celebrate the Church wedding, as we call it. We planned on doing that June 9th 2009. However, my husband and I decided we were going to have two or three kids, so we questioned, why not start before I actually graduated since most of my last year mainly involved clinical rotations. I got pregnant in March 2009, and that's where it all started.

My marvels of motherhood had just begun. We were extremely excited, so I called around for recommendations for an OB-GYN, obstetrician-gynecologist. A family friend told me to check out one particular professional. I called the doctor's office and made an appointment. I started going for my appointments and everything seemed fine. At one appointment, labs were drawn and the doctor told me my progesterone levels were low, so she put me on a progesterone shot and some other shot. Progesterone, typically called the pregnancy hormone is given to women with low levels in pregnancy. It helps to thicken the uterus and potentially decreases the chances of having a miscarriage. I went to the doctor's office every week to get those shots. She said she saw a fibroid or two in my uterus — at the time, I'd never heard of the word 'fibroid' much less have known what it was, but she insisted it wasn't anything to worry about; initially I accepted her advice and didn't worry about it.

I then had to travel to my hometown of Cameroon for the church wedding. At this time, I was almost 12 weeks pregnant, so we planned not to let anyone know about it until we returned, and I was actually showing. I scheduled my last appointment with my doctor who approved I could travel home, but she asserted that I'd have to learn how to give myself the shots. She gave me a prescription for the progesterone oil and needles as well. I filled the prescription and took it home. I had to give myself those shots more frequently than weekly, but I can't quite remember the exact dosages.

One morning my sister saw me administering the injections and asked about it. I told her I was just taking some hormones. I was going back and forth between different cities since we had to meet new people in both families and plan the wedding as well. After the wedding, my husband remained in Kumba, and I traveled to the city of Bamenda to spend some time with my family. It was special because all of us were in one house again after so many years. I slept in the same bed with my immediate older sister.

On that particular night, I experienced very mild cramps, but I ignored them at first since they weren't really painful. Everyone woke up in the morning and went downstairs to the living area. When I awoke, it was bright outside. I pulled the covers off me, and I noticed myself soaked in a pool of blood. I screamed and yelled out my sister's name, "Yvonne!" In turn, she started running from wherever she was, while I was bawling. She seemed so confused after seeing a bloody bed and my PJs all drenched in blood.

I then admitted, "I just miscarried."

She then replied, "Were you pregnant?"

"Yes, but I've lost it now," I added.

Yvonne inquired, "Does Mama know?"

I emphasized "No, I haven't told anyone."

She encouraged, "Don't cry, stay right here, and let me go get Mama."

She sprinted to get my mom, while I just got down on the floor, not knowing what to do. Mama came and she comforted me. She urged me to clean up and get dressed, because we'd need to go to the nearby hospital for a possible dilation and curettage (D&C) in case everything wasn't expelled. A D&C is simply a dilation of the cervix and scraping and scooping out any contents of the uterus.

In retrospect, we were supposed to travel to Douala that same day, but plans would have to change. Mom contacted Dad to explain the situation. After Mom called Dad, he wasn't too keen about the nearby hospital because of a previous, negative experience there which brought back bad memories, so he recommended we go downtown to a private clinic of which I'll withhold the name. At this point, I was still bleeding, so I began wearing sanitary pads. We arrived at the clinic and they performed a pregnancy test to validate that it was positive. I then began thinking to myself, *even if a woman had an abortion, wouldn't she probably still test positive, or does her Human Chorionic Gonadotropin (HCG) instantly drop?*

Chapter 2
Faith Versus Fear

"Faith is seeing light with your heart when all your eyes see is darkness."

-Barbara Johnson

This was an episode where I had to rely on my faith in the midst of chaos, death, and fear. I was swiftly admitted to the clinic and they gave me a plastic bag to place the sanitary pads in to proactively monitor how much blood was being lost. While laying on that bed, I vividly remember changing sanitary pads just about every hour. Evening arrived and Mom and I weren't too comfortable with the plan of care. My mom asked if there was an echography machine, typically called an ultrasound in the U.S. The doctor said there was none in Bamenda, and that the closest would be in Bafoussam, which was about 77km (47.8 miles) away. It's important to keep in mind how the roads aren't the best, so it could take three hours to get there.

In addition, my mom was hoping we could get an ultrasound first before proceeding with the D&C. My sister, Laura, recalled how her late father-in-law was an OB-GYN, so she talked to her mother-in-law about the situation. She mentioned how there was an ultrasound machine in his clinic. Now, it was almost 11 p.m. We decided to leave that clinic and go to her father-in-law's clinic. I had to sign some papers because I was leaving against medical advice; they wanted me to rest overnight and to avoid rough roads, as the jerking may worsen my health.

We insisted that we had to travel from the city the next day, at least, so I could be evaluated at a better clinic. We headed to Dr. Nana's clinic and Laura's mother-in-law notified the doctor, so he could be at the clinic when we got there. We arrived there by midnight; he opened up the clinic and we all eagerly awaited for what would be next. I'd been changing pads about every three hours now. I sat on the bed and he turned on the ultrasound. As a result, to everyone's utter shock, he detected a heartbeat! I knew it wasn't twins, so I was quite confused. All he said was, "The baby is alive!" That alone, gave us immense comfort. He further cautioned about any additional travel. Victor chose to meet us in Douala while he was working on moving up our tickets so I could leave for the U.S immediately. The problem was that I had to be in stable condition.

Early the next day, we left Bamenda and of course the driver couldn't drive that fast because of the roads and my condition. Thankfully, we safely got to my sister's house in Douala. My aunty then contacted a family friend with a clinic, though not an OB-GYN. He planned on admitting me to the hospital. He didn't have an ultrasound machine, but he offered to take me in and in the morning, I could get another ultrasound at his friend's clinic. At this point, I was so stressed out, yet I tried to keep calm, remain hopeful, and clutch my faith.

While at home, I went to use the bathroom and as I peed, I discharged very huge, tennis ball-like clots of blood, so I lost it again, "Yvonne!" I screamed and she ran to me. She then switched out my pad I'd just changed 15 minutes before. I told her I thought the baby was truly gone this time around. In my mind, I sincerely hoped for a better outcome, yet I prepared for the worst, unfortunately, because of what I'd just seen.

We then made our way to my aunt's family friend's clinic. He performed a cervical exam and said my cervix wasn't open at all. They admitted me and put me on some medications to prevent blood loss. I was still getting the progesterone shot and the other shot. In the morning, I went to the other clinic, and lo and behold, they still could hear a heartbeat!

I went back to the initial hospital where I remained until the day before our departure. My bleeding persisted, though somewhat reduced. We headed back to the U.S., and we immediately called my doctor and made an appointment. She checked the heartbeat, and it was still there! She scheduled my appointments once every two weeks, because I was bleeding daily. Every single day was a nightmare because I changed about eight or so pads due to heavy bleeding. I didn't know the bleeding was due to the fibroids.

On top of that, I began having very severe lower abdominal pain that was not controlled by any pain medication. Walking was almost impossible. With each gingerly step I took, it felt like a 500-pound weight was hanging on a string tied to my belly button. I was admitted at the hospital on two different occasions for a period of about three or four days. In reality, Indomethacin was the only drug that controlled my pain; but also because I was pregnant, they could only give it to me for a certain number of days as an inpatient. It relieved the excruciating pain in the short term, but when the pain came back, it came hard! Amidst the pain, I kept holding on because God chose me as a surrogate to bring forth this miracle

My dear mother-in-law had come from Cameroon and lived with us. She was going to stay and help us out with the baby once he was born. She traveled to Maryland sometime in October when I was almost 28 weeks pregnant. Before she left for Maryland, I remember her bending over to my tummy and talking to the baby, telling him she's traveling and to wait until she returns before making his debut into the world. That holy heartbeat fueled our faith!

Chapter 3
29 Weeks: The Jewel Called Jesse

"The littlest feet make the biggest footprints in our hearts."

-Unknown

A day after her departure, I remember well one night when I was asleep. I woke up to go pee and when I walked into the bathroom, I felt a gush of water go down my legs, and I knew I hadn't peed on myself. I woke Victor up abruptly and told him I thought my water broke. We headed to the hospital where they admitted me. Let me mention that earlier that day, I was driving back from my clinical rotations and was pulled over by the cops for speeding. I do not remember how far above the speed limit I was driving, but when the cop queried me I lied to him and told him I was having contractions in order to avoid getting a speeding ticket. The words we speak are powerful. They are like messengers we dispatch to execute whatever was spoken. There are therefore no casual words. Think before you speak!

At the hospital, they checked and acknowledged that yes, my water broke at 29 weeks! I was told that once your amniotic sac breaks, the baby could possibly stay in there for up to two weeks. The doctor decided she was going to monitor me, but if I started bleeding, she urged that the baby would have to be delivered.

Sometime later that night, the bleeding commenced. As God would have it, one of the Maternal Fetal Doctors later told us he was just roaming around the hospital in the middle of the night when he should have long been home. *God kept him for me!* I was rushed in, general anesthesia was given, and the baby was delivered. They realized I had a placental abruption.

My jewel arrived on October 21, 2009, weighing 2 lbs. 6oz. Most new moms would immediately hold their babies; however, I didn't get the chance to hold him right away because I was under general anesthesia and he was whisked away to the NICU (Neonatal Intensive Care Unit). We named him Jesse because he was God's gift to us, and the name also means 'God exists'. I was in my last year of Pharmacy school, and we had the month of December off. However, my instructors were understanding and excused me the rest of the month, but I had to resume school in November and December. Jesse was in the NICU for almost two months.

Chapter 4
NICU Roller Coaster

"Life can be like a roller coaster with its ups and downs. What matters is whether you are keeping your eyes open or closed during the ride and who is next to you."

— Ana Ortega

The NICU was another nightmare and roller coaster of its own. Any parent who has had babies in the NICU will understand. One second babies are doing well and the next second they go down causing parental panic. Jesse was so tiny that I didn't touch him for three days after he was born. When friends called asking how the baby was doing, I told them he looked like a rat. I remember being wheeled down to the NICU to see him that 2nd night and when I asked where he was, they said, "Right there," pointing at the incubator; however, I initially didn't see a baby in there as he was so tiny.

As I walked closer and peeked at him tears rolled down my eyes. They inquired if I wanted to hold him, and I said no. After some convincing from the evening nurse, I summoned the courage and finally touched my own son on day three and the bonding was immediate. I didn't want to put him down. I then would visit him in the NICU early before school, and then after school I'd go in and stay for extended periods where I could do kangaroo care (holding the baby skin to skin).

Victor would also go there in between my school hours. One minute, NICU babies are fine and the next day, they could have gone south. This one fateful day, the nightmare came when they called my rotation site asking where I was and telling me to come immediately to the hospital. Jesse had gotten sick. He contracted some strange bug they'd never seen, that put him down and his breathing was off. He'd take some breaths in, and then forget to breathe again. As a preemie, if he wasn't stimulated to breathe, he could just forget to breathe and eventually stop breathing altogether. My instructor let me leave immediately. I had all kinds of scary thoughts running through my mind as I drove to the hospital. On my way there, I called Victor, who just told me to come urgently.

When I got to the hospital, I noticed unusual numbers of people around his bedside. When I walked in, a few of them stepped out. I met one of his favorite nurses sitting by his bedside, pretty much rubbing his back in and out. He needed one-on-one care so they required one of us to be by his bedside to constantly remind him to breathe. I looked at my tiny boy and prayed as I sat there. He needed a blood transfusion and they wouldn't take it from Dad because he had been out of the country for the last however many years. I doubted that Dad was even the perfect blood match.

While at my rotation site, a gracious Caucasian guy from my work rotation site told me he had the unique blood type needed for babies; and if I didn't mind, he could donate some blood in Jesse's name. That same day after work, he headed over to the donation center and donated the blood in my baby's name.

Over the next few days, Jesse was able to get a blood transfusion and he got better. As he grew bigger, they were able to put clothes on him and he wore his first onesie (preemie size), which was big when he was a month old. Every NICU parent looks forward to the day when their baby will come home, and ours was no different. After about six weeks, he checked off on completing his feeds, weighed 4 lbs, and was able to maintain his temperature, so it was time to go home. We were finally bringing our precious baby home after almost two months in the NICU.

Chapter 5
My Mother-in-Love

"Then they lifted up their voices and wept again; and Orpah kissed her mother-in-law, but Ruth clung to her."

-Ruth 1:14

Reme, as we fondly called her, had returned to Oklahoma, in preparation for Jesse's coming home. She was a very soft spoken and caring lady who wouldn't hurt a fly. We understood each other very well, and unlike some daughters-in-law, we had an awesome relationship. She took great care of Jesse and life was great for all of us. I remember one fateful morning when Reme called me into the bathroom and told me she just saw blood in her stool. She showed it to me, and I didn't think much about it initially, I just told her she probably strained and there might have been a tear down there. I later told Victor about it. Being a pharmacist as well, he knew enough to be concerned more about the color of the blood, whether dark versus bright, to know where it was coming from exactly.

At another time her gums had started bleeding. Victor decided to make an appointment for her with our primary care doctor. He examined her and said he needed to send her blood work to a hematologist, just in case. The results came back and we were told Reme had Leukemia. It was at that point that life took a different turn. She had several appointments with a cancer specialist. They put her on some medications and the doctor talked to us about all the pros and cons of chemo, and we decided for the chemo because at the time it seemed to be the better option. We then broke the news to the family in the U.S and in Cameroon. We checked her into the hospital in April 2010 and chemo started.

It wasn't easy juggling between school, her hospital visits, and taking care of Jesse. By the grace of God, I was able to graduate. My hooding ceremony was on a Friday, and the most difficult thing for me was having Reme in the hospital while I went to get hooded. It was quite painful, especially the fact that she'd come from home to be with us and now wouldn't be able to attend.

After the ceremony that evening, we all drove straight to the hospital. I looked at her and struggled to hold back the tears that were filling my eyes. I knelt by her bedside, and I vividly remember giving her a hug as she squeezed my hand. Literally she took some money from her purse, placed it in my hand, and squeezed it closed as her way of saying "Congratulations." Her mouth was swollen at the time due to a tooth infection so she could barely talk yet a smile illuminated through her pale face and swollen jaw. Every time I think of that moment, even as I write this, I tear up, because it was one of the most special moments I shared with her.

All in all, she successfully went through chemo, though it changed her a lot physically and emotionally, and on the positive side, spiritually as well. She was in remission for one year. She continued follow-ups with her doctor; and after about a year and a half, the Leukemia relapsed. The physician started talking about how much time she had left and we knew things were taking a wrong turn. We decided for her to go back home— to Cameroon— and see the family during that remission phase since she had been away from home for quite some time. She had a Thanksgiving service while she was there. We were very much aware that once she returned, we were going to start some kind of treatment again.

When she arrived back to the U.S., the doctors' visits began. The second round of chemo, if we chose to, wouldn't be as successful as the first one was. When we weighed the benefits versus the risks, we decided for her to be on oral medications and not put her through that second round of chemo.

During this tumultuous time for Reme, I got pregnant with baby number two. At this point she wasn't very strong, so we still took Jesse to daycare. Like any typical African mom, one could gather that she felt bad that she was here but couldn't look after the baby; and on top of that, we had to take care of her as well.

Over time, she became weaker and weaker. Sometimes, she wouldn't eat and we'd get her Ensure and protein shakes, just so she got something in her stomach. I remember times when I'd dish her food and set it on the table covered, so she'd just have to put in the microwave and eat. I'd often return from work and her food would still be there. I'd get upset at her, asking her why she didn't eat. I even tried to force her to come eat, but I could tell she'd given up hope. She'd try, but she could barely eat, so then I'd give her a shake which she never really finished. We used to have a lot of conversations together, but those last days, she sort of avoided my conversations.

Chapter 6
Reme's Final Moments

"What we have once enjoyed deeply we can never lose. All that we love deeply becomes a part of us."

-Helen Keller

On that fateful Sunday morning in July 2011, as we were getting ready for church, she called me into her room, and she motioned that she couldn't breathe well. She could barely talk. If you knew Reme, you'd know she never liked to bother people so I realized it was serious. In turn, I rushed to the living room and to get Victor. We supported her to the car and took her immediately to the hospital. Little did we know that, that would be the last time we'd ever see her at home. She was taken into the ER, sedated, and then intubated.

When she somewhat stabilized, she was taken to ICU (Intensive Care Unit). We informed all family and friends and many of them were there for us. We'd visit her in the hospital and would talk to her. She could hear us though she couldn't respond, nor move any part of her body. Her pastor visited with her, talked to her, and I believe she was ready to cross over. However, she held on because some of the kids were in denial and kept praying.

Once Victor was able to get everyone on board to understand that she was ready to go, they all came to that agreement. Victor entered the room, relayed the message to her, and told her everyone was going to be just fine, and we didn't want her in any more pain. Well, guess what? He held her hand and she squeezed it, something she hadn't done since we checked into the hospital and took her last breath. I found peace knowing that she knew it was time to go, and she was happy since we reassured her we were all going to be fine. Like her pastor, Ron, said, "She saw that light and decided to go and walk through."

Pastor Hance had referred us to a friend who owned a funeral home. We contacted the funeral home and the director, a very nice gentleman, walked us through the process. Here we found ourselves picking out a casket for Reme! My God! This was my first experience; walking through that room looking at caskets was one of the toughest things I've ever had to deal with. We made arrangements for her corpse to be taken home to Cameroon. Since she'd lived here for a few years, we decided to have a viewing here in the U.S. I remember going from store to store, looking for the perfect outfit to dress up my sweet lady. The day before her viewing, my mom and my aunt accompanied me to the funeral home and we dressed her properly.

At the time, this was the closest person I'd ever lost, so it was tough going through the process. As a result of my condition I couldn't go home, but Victor did, accompanying her corpse. The day she was laid to rest at home in Cameroon, my life took a drastically different turn in the U.S.

Chapter 7
The Valley of the Shadow of Death

"Yea, though I walk through the valley of the shadow of death, I will fear no evil; For You are with me; Your rod and Your staff, they comfort me."

-Psalm 23:4

Since my husband had traveled home to Cameroon, my mom came to Oklahoma to help with Jesse, considering I was pregnant as well. One fateful night my cousin, Nancy, offered to spend the night with me. It was getting late that night and I wondered if she was going to come or not. At about 10 p.m. or a little later, she appeared. When preparing for bed, my mom encouraged Nancy to sleep in one of the empty rooms, instead of my bedroom. As a typical African parent in my marital home, she felt like respect should be given to our matrimonial bed; and even though Victor was away no one should be sleeping in there, not even if she was my sister. Although Nancy was my cousin, I insisted that she should sleep in the same bed as me, and so she did.

In the middle of the night, I woke up and felt funny, like I was about to pass out. I thought my blood sugar was low. I rushed to the kitchen and got a glass of orange juice and barely made my way back to the bedroom. Our mattress was kind of high, so as I tried getting back in the bed, I felt a sharp pain and I couldn't climb. Nancy was typically a deep sleeper, but somehow she heard my soft moans and turned around and asked if I was okay. I struggled to respond and said, "No, I think we need to go to the hospital!"

She jumped from bed, got my mom who woke Jesse up, and we all piled into the car. Getting me in the car was another major problem, because I couldn't lift myself up. I was hurting so badly I thought I was going to die. It felt like the contents of my stomach were being jabbed and pulled out. They got a couple of pillows to support me as they somehow just lifted me into the car. I was crying profusely.

The hospital was only 10 minutes away, and we needed to get to the hospital as fast as we could. Nancy had to be extra careful driving because every jerk made me feel like my guts were coming out of my mouth and I was in severe pain, on a scale of 1-10, the pain was at 11! Jesse was sitting in the back seat with me and cried all the way through as he watched me, while Mamma kept trying to gently calm him down. Finally, we made it to the ER - Emergency Room. They brought the wheel chair and getting me out was a nightmare; they just pulled me out of the car and I felt like they tore my stomach open!

When we got to the front desk, they asked about insurance and all as Nancy reiterated that I couldn't talk. She frantically searched my wallet while they tried to pull me up in their system and register me as well. They took me upstairs to Triage. Several nurses attempted to get an IV (intravenous) line in to no avail. They finally called the house supervisor to help. They could barely hear the baby's heartbeat, so they took me into surgery immediately. At this point I was unable to breathe, gasping for air, and my eyes were rolling back into my head;. It felt like they disappeared into the back of my forehead. They hooked me up on oxygen and it was later that I was told, my blood pressure read 60 something over 40 something. Don't ask me how I survived. As they wheeled me down to the OR (operating room), I could barely lift my hand and wave to Mamma and Nancy. In my head, I was telling them "Bye, till we meet again," because I didn't think I was going to make it out of the OR.

We often ask a lot of questions as to why certain things happen and where God was at the time. God was there! He pulled me out of that valley of the shadow of death. Nancy said she called her pastor about 2 a.m. and they were praying. The doctors were able to deliver the baby at 31 weeks, and I think she had an Apgar score of 1 or 2 out of 10. Apgar (Appearance, Pulse, Grimace, Activity, and Respiration) score is simply a measure of the physical condition of a newborn. Points of 2,1, or 0 are added for heart rate, respiratory effort, response to

53

stimulation, muscle tone and skin color. I made it out of surgery but the baby was in critical condition.

Apparently, my uterus had totally ruptured and the baby was in my stomach, which explained the pain I was having. Being in the stomach deprives the baby of oxygen, which will definitely affect brain function. If anyone knows a thing or two about uterine ruptures, you'll know it could kill mother and child, especially in severe cases like mine.

It was a couple of days before I was strong enough to go see my baby. She was intubated and all kinds of equipment attached to her. I cried when I saw her because the same machines I saw Reme hooked up to before her passing, were the same my little Nasia was hooked up to, and it just brought back all the memories. They called Victor in Cameroon and gave the news of her birth right after Reme was laid to rest, and every one rejoiced and was dancing over her grave that a baby was born, almost replacing Reme. Her middle name was after her grandma, who had just passed. At the time we did not tell them the specific circumstances surrounding her birth. Victor eventually came back to the U.S and we had to give him a summary of what happened during his three-week absence.

In sum, Nasia had no brain activity, couldn't cry, and had no gag reflex at all. She couldn't eat by mouth so she was tube fed. She was put on seizure medications due to the absence of brain activity. She was on a ventilator fighting for her life.

Chapter 8
Descent into the Darkness of Depression

"Why am I discouraged? Why is my heart so sad? I will put my hope in God! I will praise him again— my Savior and my God!"

-Psalm 42:11, NLT

Seeing all that was happening put me on a quest for knowledge. I couldn't understand. I was depressed and my heart bled on an almost daily basis. Once, when I went visiting in the NICU, one of the nurses would sit me down and ask me a few questions. She noticed there was something not right about me, so she encouraged me to also talk to my doctor. About four weeks after Nasia's birth, my OB-GYN referred me to a psychiatrist. Though reluctant, I set up an appointment because I needed help. Victor went to the appointment with me. The doctor put me on an antidepressant which I took for a couple of weeks, which led to other side effects I couldn't tolerate. Another medication was prescribed to counteract the side effects of the previous one. I took that for about two weeks as well.

I remember sitting one day at home and asking myself if this was what life was going to be like.

Sometimes I'd blank out and just stare into nothing. The medication was supposed to stir up the happy chemicals in my body. I couldn't continue taking these medications to make me happy on a daily basis. That to me, meant I would be dependent on them.

Something just wasn't right. I needed to find hope in something else. After seeing the psychiatrist for about two months, I told Victor I wanted to stop seeing him because I didn't feel he was doing me any good. The next day I called the psychiatrist's office and told them I wanted to cancel all appointments. The nurse told me if I did that, I'd have to come and sign a form in the office saying I was discharging myself against medical advice. I told her I understood that and didn't have a problem with it. The following day, I went into his office and signed the form; that was the last day I stepped foot in a psychiatrist's office. Several years later, I found out that particular psychiatrist had now become a woman, and it made me wonder who was needing more help then.

Chapter 9
Spiritual Hunger

"God releases more of His power and presence according to the measure of our hunger for Him.

-Mike Bickle

We were raised in Christian homes and we attended church every single Sunday. When I moved to the U.S, I still went to church regularly. With all this happening, I didn't understand why a good God would do something like this to my family. *Where did I go wrong?* I knew there was more to God that I needed to tap into; however, the place where I worshiped at the time didn't quite satisfy me. The best way I can explain is your mom may cook a pot of food and share among all the kids at home, and when the pot is empty you know the food is finished and you cannot ask for more, because you're certain there's nothing else at home. My situation was one where I knew there was more food in that pot and I hungered and hungered, yet it seemed no one could get in and get some out for me.

In essence, this was a very real hunger! A spiritual hunger. I was searching for something more. When you go through difficult times, people sympathize with you, but boy-oh-boy, some of the things that were said, just made it worse for me. "God won't give you what you can't handle" … then I asked myself, *Did you really give this to me Lord? "Everybody has their own cross, don't ask God why"*, *"We just have to accept it, "God giveth and God taketh"* …God didn't say that. I knew it was a statement made by Job in his pain. God didn't cause my pain!

Sympathizers will rally around you in tough times, but they merely throw pity parties and do nothing to take you out of your pain. Nothing anyone said could soothe my pain. My husband knew I wasn't a fan of traditional worship, so he had me check out another service which was more contemporary with praise and worship. I tried that and though better, it still didn't meet my needs. My cousin, Nancy, was worshiping at another church in the area, and she'd invited me a few times to their services, of which I went to a couple of times. At this moment, I decided to continue attending services at our church, and after our service was over, I'd go to hers. A month or two into going there, I started feeling somewhat refreshed.

One day I was watching TBN, and I saw Andrew Wommack appear. I just liked the way he talked and the content of what he said. By nature, I'm not a loud person, so I really connected with him. I got on the internet after that and searched for him. I realized he had a lot of free content available, so I downloaded many of his teachings on my tablet. He delivered teachings on Faith and Healing. Nasia had been between two hospitals for a little over three months, and was now discharged to go 'home'; however , we couldn't bring her home. In the state of Oklahoma it's a complicated process to get enough training for the state to approve you to take care of someone on a ventilator in your private home.

We both had full-time jobs, so our option was to put her in a long-term care facility that was about 20 minutes from home, where we could visit her daily. There was a waiting list as not many such facilities are available to serve kids that need their services. We remained at the hospital until they called saying a bed had come open then she was moved. We tried to make her area as homey as we possibly could, with a few pictures of family around. Victor bought an iPod and some speakers and we played something inspirational 24/7 by her bedside. Either gospel music was playing or the Bible. I realized that while at the NICU, and even at this facility, staff just liked being around her bedside and some even mentioned it to us. I knew it was the atmosphere we had created. You can take charge of your atmosphere and be the thermostat, not the thermometer. I've also learned that circumstances may not be favorable around you, but it's how you respond to those situations that will determine whether you sink or float. The ball is in your court.

In such circumstances don't allow people to determine how you feel. People will come around you and want to throw a pity party for you because they really do care but it doesn't help you because the minute they're gone, you're alone. It's like they walk with you to the middle of a bridge and leave you there. It's people who are filled with compassion that will take you all the way to the other end of the bridge. Every single day, one of us was at the Children's Facility to visit with Nasia. The pastor of the church where we worshiped came over and dedicated her at the facility's chapel. We took Jesse there as often as we could and he just loved his sister.

Every time I was there, I'd listen to Andrew Wommack's teachings which really built my faith and I realized that God wasn't the author of sickness and disease. As I grew my faith, I didn't understand why people would pray for her, yet leave it up to God, by saying things like "If it is your will" when He has given us the power to heal. If one does not know the will of God on any issue, it is impossible for Him to have faith. It therefore is His will for us to be healed and walk in Divine health. However, I wasn't really surrounded by many people who believed this concept.

Chapter 10
My Trials, Tribulations, & Tongues

"And they were all filled with the Holy Spirit and began to speak with other tongues, as the Spirit gave them utterance."

-Acts 2:4

I found out Andrew Wommack was coming to Houston for one of his Gospel Crusade tours. I got excited and really wanted to go, but I'd have to discuss it with my husband. He said it was okay to go so I planned ahead and bought my ticket, and I was going to be there only on Saturday. I got to Houston on a Friday; my cousin, Nina picked me up from the airport and we went to the crusade on Saturday. While I was at the crusade, I really felt good. He took the stage and began teaching. Towards the end, he got to the gift of speaking in tongues. This was a topic I never liked just because it was that gibberish thing I didn't believe in initially. I mean, *where's it coming from?* I remember him asking those who wanted that gift to come forward. I told myself I can't say I want all of God, yet choose the things I do want and the things that I don't want. I told God that if this 'tongues' thing was indeed Him, I wanted it by all means.

I made that hesitant walk to the altar as I still wasn't sure if it was real or not. *Could it be I was being initiated into a cult? Or is it really God?* I lifted up my hands as others were doing. After about five minutes of prayers, he invited us to begin and just let it out. After another five minutes, he asked those who received it to raise their hands, and quite a few people did. I didn't and began to wonder why. They closed the service and informed those of us who came forward to proceed to a room for a free gift— a book— that would teach us more about our new language. I walked in and sat at the back. My eyes moved so fast in every angle as I quickly scanned through to see who was in there. It was obvious I was still wondering what I'd signed up for. I was handed a book, and I took it. Although I didn't speak in tongues then, the conference was still a blessing to me.

On Sunday, I left to return to Oklahoma. Two weeks after I got back to Oklahoma, I decided to read the book. As soon as I closed that book, *The New you and the Holy Spirit,* I got on my knees and just began to thank God aloud for the new gift He had given me, since I received it by faith.

Suddenly, I began to say things that I didn't understand and that of course sounded like gibberish. It was like a river of gibberish bursting out of my stomach and through my mouth. I started crying because I couldn't believe it happened. I kept going on for a while.

I didn't tell anyone, not even Victor. Keep in mind that our church was very conservative and didn't believe in speaking in tongues, nor did I ever really hear a message on healing, our God given right. When you begin speaking in tongues, the enemy doesn't leave you alone, and I think we were cautioned about that — slightly— in the book. What lie didn't he— the enemy— tell me ? It was from the devil! It wasn't really God. I was opening myself up to demonic things, with him saying I was the one making up stuff and not the Holy Spirit speaking through me. I got scared and for some months I didn't really exercise the gift. I was therefore not fluent in the Heavenly language I'd just received because I didn't put it into practice.

Chapter 11
Through It All: Saying *Adieu* to Nasia

"For in grief nothing "stays put." One keeps on emerging from a phase, but it always recurs. Round and round. Everything repeats. Am I going in circles, or dare I hope I am on a spiral? But if a spiral, am I going up or down it How often -- will it be for always? -- how often will the vast emptiness astonish me like a complete novelty and make me say, "I never realized my loss till this moment"? The same leg is cut off time after time."

-C.S. Lewis

With an almost three-year-old child and working full time, it wasn't easy going back and forth visiting Nasia in that facility, but somehow God gave us the strength. Friends and family visited her while she was in there. One would think that every time I saw her, my spirits would go down; however, it was just the opposite. I may have a long day at work or maybe I'm just not having it that day, but when I stop by to see Nasia, I'd leave her bedside feeling more energetic than ever. Nesting with Nasia wasn't like the traditional parental bonding, but those memories are forever etched in my heart.

Nasia contracted an infection, which is pretty common with kids in a facility. It affected her breathing, which wasn't very strong in the first place, causing major fluctuations in her temperatures. She was on antibiotics, and just kept declining over the week. She didn't respond like she normally would when I visited with her. I got a call one fateful morning and they said she wasn't doing well and urged me to come over immediately. Victor called me and we decided to meet there. Victor got there before me; however, by the time we arrived she had passed away minutes before in the Nurse Practitioner's arms.

I saw the Nurse Practitioner sitting in the recliner and I gazed at my lifeless baby in her arms. I'm tearing up as I write this because it isn't a story I've ever recounted. The news had spread fast throughout the facility so most of her caregivers stepped in to see her for a last time. They all assured us her passing on was peaceful and she was relaxed and in no pain. That gave me some comfort and though the enemy tried to play mind games with me not being there, no one, not even me, could dispute the love we showed Nasia, and she knew it.

Victor took our baby from the Nurse Practitioner and I watched her peaceful body resting in his arms. I hugged them both and we traded places as I held her lifeless body and just kept kissing on her. I leaned forward, kissed her forehead and I asked God to give me a peace that passes all understanding. I told God I was certain He did not cause this, but I knew good would come out of it. Victor stepped out to call the same funeral home he'd dealt with some months earlier when his mom passed. I didn't even want to imagine what was going through his own mind. I called a dear sister-friend and gave her the news. She came there and was with me for some time, while Victor communicated with the rest of the family.

I gently put Nasia back in her bed and covered her up lovingly. The funeral director appeared and the look on his face was like "Oh no!" I found myself in a position where I had to be strong for others.

The following week, we laid precious Nasia to rest. I didn't want her in white. I just wanted her as a little girl. I may have dressed her in light pink or so, I don't quite remember. Family and friends came from across the U.S. Within me, I knew it wasn't God's will for Nasia to die at such a young age of six months. However, I knew all things work together for good for them that love the Lord (Romans 8:28). I didn't want her funeral to be sad. I know that sounds funny, like 'It's a funeral-duh!' What I mean was I wanted people, including us, to find hope in the midst of it all. I wanted everyone to know that there still is hope. The program was intentionally designed with specific verses and songs. I had them play one song that ministered to me through this trying time. It was composed by Andrae Crouch and goes:

JEHOVAH HAS HEALED

Verse 1

I've had many tears and sorrows,
I've had questions for tomorrow,
There's been times I didn't know right from wrong.
But in every situation,
God gave me blessed consolation,
that my trials come to only make me strong.

Chorus

Through it all,
Through it all,
I've learned to trust in Jesus,
I've learned to trust in God.
Through it all,
through it all,
I've learned to depend upon His Word.

Verse 2

I've been to lots of places,
I've seen a lot of faces,
there's been times I felt so all alone.
But in my lonely hours,
yes, those precious lonely hours,
Jesus lets me know that I was His own.

Chorus

Verse 3

I thank God for the mountains,
and I thank Him for the valleys,
I thank Him for the storms He brought me through.
For if I'd never had a problem,

I wouldn't know God could solve them,
I'd never know what faith in God could do.

In essence, I remember Pastor Hance saying, during his sermon, that he came to encourage us and give us hope, but the reverse happened instead. Many people gave testaments to the fact that their faith was challenged. Several people who attended the funeral returned a different— better way— than they came. That surely blessed me through it all and helped in saying *Adieu* to Nasia!

Chapter 12
Unmasked: Healing After Bereavement

"Grief is like the ocean; it comes on waves ebbing and flowing. Sometimes the water is calm, and sometimes it is overwhelming. All we can do is learn to swim."

-Vicki Harrison

Life gradually got back to a new normal after Nasia's passing. Over the next few weeks and even over the year I'd visit her grave quite frequently, almost daily, sometimes with flowers. I'd hang out there for some minutes, look up to the sky, often weep, get into my car, and drive back home. We'd typically go there on Memorial Day as well.

One day, I had a revelation and it seemed the Holy Spirit was asking me why I kept going to her grave. I honestly didn't have an answer. I began to question myself if I was just doing it because I see other people do it. The more I thought about it, the more I realized it added nothing positive for me. It didn't give me any more faith than I had nor did it revive my spirit. If anything, it made me sadder, and I sure didn't like that feeling. It seemed like a bondage I'd unconsciously put myself into with no headway of breaking free.

I asked God to take away my pain, and that I was going to fully depend on Him. I implored him to delete death dates from my mind as well. Paul tells us in **Philippians 4:8-9**

"8 Finally, brethren, whatever things are true, whatever things are noble, whatever things are just, whatever things are pure, whatever things are lovely, whatever things are of good report, if there is any virtue and if there is anything praiseworthy—meditate on these things. 9 The things which you learned and received and heard and saw in me, these do, and the God of peace will be with you."

None of those things I did had released the peace of God in me. If anything, I was able to release some tears. It felt good, yet hurt; for how long was I going to keep crying? She was with God in glory, not in the grave. That will be like a Christian going to the tomb where Jesus was every single day and crying when we have a risen Savior. Once I stopped doing those visits, I felt some kind of liberation in my spirit.

Grief shouldn't be a parade. I see several people do stuff like this nowadays, especially on social media, and it makes me wonder if they're doing it because they see other people do it and feel like it needs to be emulated. Grief cuts so deep that sometimes one does or says certain things without even thinking. Some who have lost loved ones get on Facebook, Instagram, Twitter, Snap chat etc. and tell the world how it's the 3rd, 10th,

23rd, 39th or whatever year since the passing of their loved one; some say they remember it like yesterday, and then friends come and comment under these posts, sympathizing with or encouraging the individual and all. This happens on a yearly basis. I'm all for celebrating the wonderful lives our loved ones had on earth, whether long or short. However, I've discovered that some people do so to call attention to themselves on these anniversary days. To them, getting all the attention on such posts sort of makes them feel good. You can definitely remember your loved one any and every single day of the week, but to subject oneself to such mandatory yearly remembrances isn't my cup of tea. I also know a few people who on that day yearly, they'd spend their entire day crying, or maybe doing things the loved one enjoyed doing and just remembering them in one way or another.

In contrast, I believe healing is different for everyone and is a process. It won't happen overnight. However, if after so many years, you truly do feel the pain like it happened yesterday, then you need to invite Jesus to help you heal completely. As 1 Thessalonians 4:13 tells us not to grieve like people who have no hope. We know that we'll see them again, so it isn't for us to let the enemy play these tricks with us year by year. They've passed on to glory and live better lives than they did while here, so I celebrate that and unmask my bereavement and head toward healing!

Chapter 13
Growing Wings: My Growth Period

"When we refuse to go through the process, we resist growth."

-Carine Njoh

After Nasia's passing, I felt a void. I was still trying to recover from Reme's passing, just six months before, and processing that when Nasia passed away. How do I deal with this one? I cried many times. I mourned for Jesse, wondering if he'd ask questions. I'd dismissed the psychiatrist so I knew I was on my own. I began searching here and there. Lord, I need help, I prayed. I even went on Amazon to look for books to answer some of my questions. My passion for reading grew and I pursued it fervently.

I remember my cousin had invited me to her church a couple of times and so I decided to visit that church again. Like I said earlier, I felt revived when I attended their services. Since Victor and I worshiped together at another non-Pentecostal church, I'd continue to go with him on Sundays and after the first service, I'd drive to Miracle City for their services. I did that for such a long time, a little over a year, and it just got to a point where he was like, "I think you enjoy services better there, so you can just go on." I planted myself there. They held services three times a week: Sunday services, midweek teaching service/Bible study and on Fridays, Prayer Mountain. I made sure I attended every service as long as I wasn't working.

A little over a year after Nasia's passing, I got pregnant again. We were building our new home and so we were very busy going back and forth checking on the new property. We had sold our house before the new one was finished, so we moved into an apartment, where we would be for about three months. One night I had a dream where I bled a lot on the bed. Of course, I didn't know what I know now, so I just woke up, prayed a simple prayer, and that was it. We were both very excited, especially when we found out it was going to be a girl. God had answered our prayers!

One fateful evening when Victor had gone to work, I was home with Jesse. I felt slight pains underneath my abdomen, but it wasn't that bad. I felt I could handle it with Tylenol. I took Tylenol and went to bed. Early the next morning, when Victor got back from work, the pains were so unbearable I said I had to go to the hospital. We got into the car and he drove as fast as possible. He called one of my friends, and my cousin, Nancy, and told all of them we were headed to the hospital. I thought I was going to die. My doctor then showed up on the triage floor and he knew exactly what was happening. They frantically tried to find a heartbeat, as they prepared me for surgery. Once they found one, though not strong, they rushed me in immediately. I had a uterine rupture, and gave birth to Eliana at 31 weeks. She was born with an Apgar score of 1, I believe, with 10 being the highest. Later I was told she didn't cry and they couldn't find a heartbeat.

They were going to announce her demise when she gave a breath. I cried and cried and cried. I initially blamed myself for not going to the hospital that night since I felt a little pain. I looked for answers and still couldn't find any. I questioned God as to why He would do this to me. For some reason, even though I still didn't discover answers to my questions, God was still the only One I could hold onto then. I took comfort in the fact that there was a reason for her giving that breath before they pronounced her dead. I really believed God had a purpose.

Chapter 14
Walking by Faith

"To one who has faith, no explanation is necessary. To one without faith, no explanation is possible."

-St. Thomas Aquinas

All in all, Eliana was in the hospital for six months, until she was discharged sometime in March. She was in between two hospitals and also had a tracheostomy tube, due to no muscle tone, and a G-tube. She could do nothing on her own. Muscle tone was very minimal. She never really had her eyes open; plus, if she did, it was more of a lazy eye. When we were discharged from the hospital, we were approved for home health care since we needed a nurse seven days a week, 12 hours a day. Getting approved for that is one thing, and actually having the nurses show up is another. We came home and still didn't have a nurse for almost two months. We both worked full time while taking care of our son, too. *How did we do it?* I still don't know. The grace of God.

Specifically, Eliana needed 24-hour complete care. We had to suction her around the clock depending on how frequent her secretions were. On a very good night,

I could get three hours of straight sleep, and that was very rare. Victor worked seven nights on and seven nights off. When he was off and wasn't working, he'd sometimes give me a break in the night. However, for any of us to really get some uninterrupted sleep, we'd have to sleep out of our room, where we had her bed, because of the noise of some of the machines that were running in the room. I bathed her every day, sometimes in the day and other times in the evening, depending on my schedule. There were times where she got an infection and I'd have to suction her about every 15 minutes, then would have to go to work in the morning.

We had Mom come over here and help out. Then the Home Health Care was able to find a nurse who would do three days a week. Besides dealing with all of Eliana's issues, Home Health Care was another nightmare all together. They may hire a nurse today, and she might just not show up. We also experienced others who would work for one day and never come back. Some would call in on the day of one's shift and others just wouldn't come. We've had to cancel our own appointments because a nurse didn't follow through. We took the best care of Eliana that we possibly could given the situation we were in at the time. We would go together to take her to her doctors' appointments because of the amount of equipment that would have to accompany her.

In particular, one time she fell sick and had difficulties breathing and we had to bag— squeezing of a bag to help breathing— her. We called 911. I am certified in CPR, Cardio Pulmonary Resuscitation, and for the first time in all these years, my daughter was the first person I performed CPR on. The dispatcher walked me through giving her chest compressions and rescue breaths. When the ambulance arrived she was rushed to the hospital. She was admitted in the PICU, Pediatric Intensive Care Unit. We were there for about a month. The doctors were reluctant to send her home when it came time for her to be discharged. The doctor recommended that she be placed in a facility because she couldn't breathe without a ventilator. He said if he discharged us to return home, we'd return to the hospital before the weekend. If we did bring her back in, the team of doctors and the state would likely override our will and determine what was in the best interest for Eliana.

In turn, we stubbornly—or, I'll say by faith— decided to take her home without the ventilator. The first few days were a struggle, but we made it through that weekend and for the next year and a half, she didn't have to go back to the hospital. Just like you and I would catch a cold, Eliana sometimes did as well, and those weeks were tough! Since she had a tracheostomy tube, I'd change it out weekly and so when sick, secretions multiplied. In other words, we had to blow her nose for her by suctioning. Her secretions may have to be suctioned every 15 minutes or so when sick; otherwise, she became occluded to the point she couldn't breathe at all.

I'd sit in the recliner next to her bed half asleep, with Jesse in my bed, and I'd doze off for a little bit, then wake up and suction once I heard the bubbles… which at that point had already started building up. Sometimes, I'd drink coffee, just to be awake. Then come morning, I'd get Jesse ready for school and once Victor returned home, I'd then get ready for work so we could trade places and off I would head to work. If there wasn't a nurse coming, a friend might watch her for a few minutes, while Victor rushed Jesse to school. Once he got back, he'd watch Eliana and go to sleep after I got home. I don't know how we did it, but I keep saying it was by the grace of God, a growth lesson in faith as we were growing our wings.

Chapter 15
When Affliction Rises Again

"What do you conspire against the Lord?
He will make an utter end of it.
Affliction will not rise up a second time."

-Nahum 1:9

Throughout Eliana's stay at home, reading became my passion as I also found new truths in the Bible. I dove deeper and deeper into the Word of God. Sometimes, I'd just let the Bible play throughout the night or have worship music on. Jesse loved reading to her. When we were around, she'd respond in a way we just knew she knew we were there for her. She knew her brother's voice. He asked many questions and I believe God gave me the wisdom to answer him. He'd see Eliana as uniquely made by God. Never was he ever ashamed of her. He'd tell everyone at school about his sister and how God made her special. I did not want his perception of God all twisted up because of what his sister looked like . I told him about the enemy being the origin of all evil, but that God's goodness surpasses all.

In my quest for answers, my passion for God led me to attend several conferences around the U.S, and I still attend them to learn about spreading the love of God to others, especially His healing. Over time, after about 2.5 years, Eliana began using her oxygen compressor more frequently than she normally would. Oxygen wasn't something she used on a regular basis; we just had a tank at home for when the need arose. We prayed and fasted for Eliana. Many people did. It was during these moments of fasting that I felt God strengthen me. It got to the point that when I prayed I told God, I believed in healing; however, if Eliana wasn't going to get better, I didn't want her to have to live like this.

After one of the times I fasted I had a dream. In the dream, I was at Eliana's funeral. I woke up from the dream, that seemed so real, cried and rebuked such a thing from happening. A few weeks later, I had a closed vision, and the Lord showed me the same picture I'd had in that dream. I wept and wept; it was at this point that I knew Eliana was not going to make it. The Lord clearly showed it to me and the impression in my spirit was so strong. I didn't know who to talk to at the time. I couldn't tell Victor such a dream, when we were believing God for her healing. Oh yes, I really did believe one day she'd just get up and walk!

As she deteriorated it became very difficult taking care of her at home. Her need for constant care began wearing on us since home nursing was not something we could really depend on. We talked about placing her into a facility temporarily until we sorted some things out.

Deep down in me I knew Eliana wasn't going to make it out of there. I was so scared, thinking about how I'd face the inevitable and I kept it to myself. We explained to Jesse about her going in to the facility and that come Fall, he may not be able to see her as frequently as he wanted to due to the restrictions on kids visiting during flu season.

We took her there maybe late July, early August. We talked to her at home and let her know exactly where we were taking her. As soon as she got in there, Eliana didn't like it. Her first night was rough. I told her one of us would be there at least once daily and I promised to come give her warm baths. She slowly deteriorated and increasingly became dependent on oxygen over the next four weeks or so. One fateful day, over a month after her admission, they called me and said they've had to bag her about three times and they couldn't keep doing that, as they didn't have the staff to continue. I called Victor at work, and he made arrangements to come meet me at the facility. I contacted my sister-friend to meet me there so she could take Jesse with her. I explained to Jesse what was going on and told him to kiss her and all.

Deep down I knew the time had come; it was just a matter of exactly when. We walked into her room, I cuddled her, talked to her and, comforted her. Victor came in and did the same. The facility insisted we go to one hospital, maybe because they automatically sent all their patients there, but because of a bad experience we had previously had at that hospital with her, we decided to call the other hospital directly and inquire if a bed was available. When they gave Victor the go ahead we decided to go there. We were by her bedside the whole time. We talked to her, told her what a blessing she'd been to us, and reassured her that we were all going to be okay by God's grace. The following morning, Victor had to leave to take Jesse to school. Since we had already explained the situation to him, he did his goodbye kisses and all and knew there was a possibility she'd likely soon go to be with her Maker. A couple of friends and family stopped by to see her, including my pastor. She had one of those moments in the hospital and we didn't bag her.

Victor held her in his arms, and I leaned on them both and I kissed her. Finally, he rocked her, as she gasped for air and then calmly slipped away. We both cried because it did hurt, but somehow I felt a peace within me. I can't explain it. I gave her a final bath and we left the hospital and made funeral arrangements. For the 3rd time in five years, Victor made that dreaded phone call to the same funeral director. When the guy saw me, I could sense his pain.

When I prayed, I just remembered the Lord assured me each time that He would always hold my hand. It was so funny when Jesse kept asking before she passed, "Did Eliana go to Heaven yet?" as though he was waiting. We wrestled with whether he needed to see her body or not, but we eventually did let him see her whole body, so we didn't get questions later, and I remember him saying, "Momma, Eliana is sooo cute. She's beautiful!" and I said, "Yes, sweetheart, she is. She's jumping around in Heaven now, with the other little kids."

Overtime, I had to remind him he had another sister in Heaven as well because I didn't want him to hear from some other person. We planned her funeral shortly after, and there I was again at the funeral home, dressing a third body (including my late mother-in-law) in five years! *God, where are you? What on earth am I here for?* I asked. He was silent, and sometimes in His silence, is when He speaks the loudest if only we key in and listen. At the service I did exactly what God had told me to do in the dream and closed vision, which was unlike me. I addressed the crowd without a script. Eliana was laid to rest close to her sister. It's been over a year and as I write this, I haven't been back to the cemetery. However, I know there are two beautiful souls watching down from above. I don't say angels, because we're above angels. The Bible tells us that when we die we don't become angels; instead, we take on another glorious body.

The Sunday following her funeral, we decided to do a Thanksgiving service at church. You may question the purpose of a Thanksgiving in such a time as this. I honestly didn't see any better way to give the enemy a slap in the face than to respond this way. It really confuses him. I also put together, and made sure everyone else at home did, a good offering to give unto the Lord. Praising God in the face of a challenge invites Him on scene to go before you which is already a clear indication of victory. It is us raising the banner of victory even before the battle is fought. We see in 2 Chronicles 20 where the Ammonites and Moabites came to battle against King Jehoshaphat. Jehoshaphat was initially afraid of the multitude of people they were faced with until the word of the Lord came telling him not to fear, for the battle was the Lord's.

2 Chronicles 20:17-18:

17 You will not need to fight in this battle. Position yourselves, stand still and see the salvation of the Lord, who is with you, O Judah and Jerusalem!' Do not fear or be dismayed; tomorrow go out against them, for the Lord is with you."

18 And Jehoshaphat bowed his head with his face to the ground, and all Judah and the inhabitants of Jerusalem bowed before the Lord, worshiping the Lord.

After Jehoshaphat consults with the people, he appoints those who will sing to the Lord and those who will praise the beauty of His holiness. They went before the army singing, and the Bible tells us that when they *began* to sing and praise Him, the Lord himself set ambushes against Moab, Ammon and Mount Seir who had all come against Judah and they were defeated. How powerful a weapon praise is!

I am also a firm believer that praise in tough times, breaks foundations of anything that may be keeping you bound. We can clearly see that in the scriptures.

Acts 16:23-34

23 And when they had laid many stripes on them, they threw them into prison, commanding the jailer to keep them securely. 24 Having received such a charge, he put them into the inner prison and fastened their feet in the stocks.

25 But at midnight Paul and Silas were praying and singing hymns to God, and the prisoners were listening to them. 26 Suddenly there was a great earthquake, so that the foundations of the prison were shaken; and immediately all the doors were opened and everyone's chains were loosed. 27 And the keeper of the prison, awaking from sleep and seeing the prison doors open, supposing the prisoners had fled, drew his sword and was about to kill himself. 28 But Paul called with a loud voice, saying, "Do yourself no harm, for we are all here."

29 Then he called for a light, ran in, and fell down trembling before Paul and Silas. 30 And he brought them out and said, "Sirs, what must I do to be saved?"

31 So they said, "Believe on the Lord Jesus Christ, and you will be saved, you and your household." 32 Then they spoke the word of the Lord to him and to all who were in his house. 33 And he took them the same hour of the night and washed their stripes. And immediately he and all his family were baptized. 34 Now when he had brought them into his house, he set food before them; and he rejoiced, having believed in God with all his household.

In this passage, we can see the power of praise. In verse 25, the sentence begins with 'but', which means something contrary happened. It was at midnight, they should have been asleep, but they were singing and we are told the prisoners heard them, so they didn't sing under their breath. It was in their darkest hour that they offered praises to God. When they did that, the foundations of the prison were shaken. Likewise, when you and I go through challenges, we must learn to praise God in the midst of it all. In your darkest hour, sing a new song unto the Lord. Though you may not physically see what is happening, those wrong foundations are being broken in the spiritual realm. Eventually, the physical will catch up with the spiritual.

Chapter 16
Battlefield in My Mind

"What you think, you believe, and what you believe you become"

-Carine Njoh

In most African cultures, when such tragic events repeatedly occur, people begin to come up with different reasons as to why the person is dealing with so much tragedy. The woman, for the most part, is always to blame. Some people said there were certain things I was supposed to do as a married woman that I failed to do, so I must retrace my steps. Another said in pidgin English, "If you nova touch bitter leaf, your hands them no go bitter;" meaning, if you didn't touch dirt, your hands won't get dirty. However, I knew too well that one did not have to cause trouble for trouble to come after them. So much was said that I can't even get into.

What you think, you believe, and what you believe, you become. At some point, I began to believe the lie I kept telling myself: that it seemed I was susceptible to bad luck. *Was I born to just keep experiencing pain?* Regardless of what I did, why did it just seem to be lurking around me? Two things delivered me from this toxic mindset: intense prayers at home and at church, as well as a book I came across by Wendy Alec called *Visions from Heaven: Visitations to My Father's Chamber.* After reading that book, I became convinced God indeed knew what I was going through. I felt a strange, but great love from the Father. I also made sure I didn't miss a Prayer Mountain session at church; and each time, I felt lighter than when I went in.

A year before Eliana passed, I was scheduled for a myomectomy-fibroid removal, and when the doctor went in to take it out, he realized I had a ruptured appendix as well. I remember I had felt pain in my right lower abdomen for about two years, but I just assumed it may be fibroid pain. When the doctor went in there he said my intestines were so wrapped up he didn't understand how I was able to tolerate the pain for so long and how it didn't turn into something major. I was just happy the Lord was watching over me all the while.

Grief is a tough thorn. Although I'm a very private person, I remember a minister of the Gospel saying our faith is private, but not personal. I can't erase my story, but I can embrace it and choose to tell it because I use it all for His glory. My deep encounters with God started after these experiences I had endured. We must learn to embrace our pain, because the pain you embrace will become a part of your process. Overtime, I also learned to quit asking God why, and just responded positively to the situation I was facing. In essence, I had to be forward looking. I made a decision to be full of joy regardless of what was happening.

After all this, I kind of shut myself away. I wasn't depressed or anything. I just needed a break from everything but God. Sometimes I'd feel like all eyes were on me and people began to feel sorry for me and I hated pity parties, so I avoided them at all costs. I realized I'd have to rise above all I had been through. This couldn't be it in my life. I knew God *allows* things to happen to us, but He doesn't cause evil in our lives. The Bible tells us that whenever the enemy comes it is to cause havoc. He has a tripartite ministry— To kill, steal and destroy (John 10:10). I was therefore more than convinced that though God didn't author the evil, He specializes in bringing good out of unpleasant situations.

I decided to just take a break from trying to get pregnant again. I realized that my only hope was Jesus, so I continued studying the Word day and night. I chose to read the Bible and pray that a revelation would just come. I actually began to believe what I read in those pages. I couldn't understand why these things happened to me, but I decided I was going to trust God all the same. What else did I have to lose, you know.

Chapter 17
More Hunger for God

"If you aren't hungry for God, you are full of yourself. That's why God cannot fill you with His Spirit. But if you will empty yourself, if you will die to self, you'll be a different person by the time you reach the last page of this book."

"To hunger is to be human, but to hunger for God is to feed on Him."

-Mark Batterson

I remember the very first time I tangibly felt the touch of the Holy Spirit; I wasn't even expecting anything at the time. All I had was a hunger for God. I later realized that when you hunger for God, the Holy Spirit will feed you. Sometime in 2014, December I believe, there was a three-day program at church called Divine Acceleration. I don't remember if it was the first or second day, but the Holy Spirit took a hold of my legs and my legs began to shake non-stop. I knew something good was happening, though I couldn't understand it. Even when I tried to stop it, I couldn't. At the end of the service, I started hitting my legs to try to stop it, and my mom told me to just let it be. Much later the vibrations stopped.

After this transformative incident I began to see God in a whole new dimension. I liked what happened to me, but I couldn't explain it. It felt good. The Lord gradually began to work on me. My hunger and thirst for the things of God continued. I enjoyed sharing the word of God with people and on social media. I just felt compelled to give hope to people. I realized that there were now many things I was exposed to that I hadn't been before. I began to enjoy my Christian walk, and I wanted others to enjoy the same.

Accordingly, my sleeping, my waking, my thoughts throughout the day, were all focused on God. Then the pastor organized a three-day Easter program in April 2016, called Floodgates of Heaven. On one or two of those days, I had another encounter with God. I'm an introvert by nature, but I knew it was God because the kinds of experiences I was having were ones that you knew I wouldn't display in my right state of mind. The encounters were so dramatic that I would flip my hands up and down with lots of jerky movements that would push me to the floor. When the Holy Spirit comes upon you, just like it did on the day of Pentecost, some may think you're drunk. *"For these are not drunk, as you suppose, since it is only the third hour of the day."* according to Acts 2:15. I was inebriated with the Holy Ghost, not wine. Whatever was going on with me or another person at that time, may have looked weird, but like I tell people, if that's what weird is it didn't start with me; it started with the disciples on the day of Pentecost!

The encounters continued sometimes at home, other times at church. There was a time at church when the Holy Spirit took a hold of me. The choir kept on singing and suddenly, I heard singing that seemed to have burst through the ceiling from top to bottom. It sounded like over five thousand voices that were singing in unison to the song the choir sang. Then the Holy Spirit ministered to me that it was the angels singing along with us. Such beautiful voices!

My hunger to experience God continued to grow and I began hunting for more conferences to go to. I attended Randy Clark's Global Awakening conference in 2016 in Pennsylvania. The more I drank, the more I thirsted. In the physical, the more you eat, the fuller you become, but in the spiritual realm, the more you feed on the things of God, the hungrier you become. The one major encounter that I will never forget happened when I went to Michael & Jessica Koulianous' Jesus'16 Conference in December 2016. I'd planned on attending the conference as I'd seen the flyer on Facebook. I fasted on that Monday and Tuesday until 6 p.m. in preparation for the program, as I was very expectant. I repeatedly told myself I wouldn't go to Orlando and return the same way. I arrived that Wednesday at about 2 p.m.; a friend picked me up, and I checked into my hotel. We made it to the Conference Center at about 6 p.m., though registration had opened at 5 p.m. I registered and we later made our way into the hall. The moment I walked in I was very excited. The energy in the hall was incredible! It was supercharged with Holy Ghost electricity.

Chapter 18
Ecstasy

The love of God should electrify us, push us to hunger, and stir a fiery passion in our bones that cannot be quenched. Consistent lack of emotion in our spiritual walk can often be defined in one simple word: complacency." "Don't look to wine for your stimulation. That leads only in the direction of ruin."

-John Crowder

Specifically, Daniel Kolenda was the first speaker. We were led into a time of worship, and I got slain in the spirit. Day 2, I got slain in session three while my friend, Atsi, saw a flame of fire. In the evening Brian Guerin took the stage and the worship was so beautiful that I knew I was in the presence of God. We sang in tongues, and for the first time, my tongues changed and I worshipped so well in the spirit. I got slain, and this time around I fell hard to the floor, went straight down, and hit my head really hard, it hurt for like half a second, then I felt like the Holy Spirit or some angel wrapped their arms around me. I started saying things in tongues and also uttered, "I will go," "Fire," "Burn," and then I launched into bouts of laughter. My friend said the usher kept motioning me with her hand to let more out and I did.

When I went back to the hotel Thursday night, I noticed a burning or tingling sensation around my waist, tummy and back. I brushed it off and thought it would go away eventually. I woke up the next morning and it was still there. The sensation came and went away at will and I described it as a belt with a bunch of ants on my waist.

Session 9 came along on Friday, December 9th with Eric Gilmour. We went into Heavenly worship, it was beautiful and I screamed in loud bursts, and I was taken out of the hall. Session 10 on the same night was led by Michael Koulianos, we had a great time in worship as well. I remember saying 'ssssssss', followed by deep breaths, then got slain as I articulated some words. I was taken out of the hall, and a member of the Bethel team named Malcolm, probably in his late 60's, said he heard God tell him to show me the Father's love. Another usher came to help along with a lady volunteer called Rosa, who told me she saw in the spirit a bubbled pen and saw me scribbling stuff and knew I'd write a book. She said I was a wonderful lady.

As I continued crying, I remember Malcolm holding me with a Father's touch and told me God really loved me. He gave me a kiss on my forehead, saying He had never done that. They asked if I had any pain or was dealing with something in the past, and Atsi told them I had two kids that had passed into glory. They prayed more with me, and he told me about having lost his wife five years earlier. He revealed how he'd heard God tell him to move to Bethel from another country, and He did. He reiterated that the Lord had asked him to share Romans 8:28 with me, and when He stated that, I smiled.

My husband and I had wrist bands with that inscription. Thankfully, I'd left mine at home; otherwise, I would have thought it was not God, that he saw it on my wrist. Then came Rosa, too, with the same scripture, telling me God was going to use me in a mighty way. I later told her that was the password for some of my online accounts. I went back into the hall. Some minutes later, I burst into bouts of laughter again.

My flight was taking off at 5:55 p.m. that day. Atsi and I had planned on attending the first two sessions then we'd depart, because we'd already packed our bags and checked out of the hotel. When we sat in the hall, I unconsciously, spirit led, said we were going to have to still come and queue up for the evening session with Benny Hinn. Then Atsi brought my attention to what I'd said. Immediately, I knew I had to be present for the evening session. We stepped out, made some calls and got our tickets changed.

Lastly, Benny Hinn was the speaker for the final night. At some point while he was teaching, I started breathing rapidly, then slowly, then words could not come out of my lips. My legs wouldn't move and my hands were stuck—frozen— in the position in which I had them. Three ushers came by and they wanted to take me out, but they realized I couldn't move. Rosa sat to my left and another person stooped to my right, as they tried to calm me down. I was so scared! I couldn't believe it. I tried to move my fingers, but they refused to budge.

After a few minutes, my right hand gave way, then my right leg. After about 15 or so minutes, my left knuckles popped as I tried moving my fingers, so they sat me up. Right after that happened, Benny Hinn was talking about the different levels of the anointing and explained how it happened to him a few times, usually in his bedroom. He talked about the experience of freezing and one having the feeling of almost dying, and my eyes popped open as I nodded and listened intently. Unbeknownst to me, ten minutes after that I had another experience. I froze completely, neck to feet. Left hand up, fingers spread out, right hand down. Several ushers came and carried me out while my body was straightened out, rigid and flat! Frozen. I opened my eyes and I was in the hotel kitchen. I heard the paramedics were called. I had difficulty taking breaths in and out.

However, I wasn't in pain. I don't know if I was in or out of my body, but I sort of knew everything that was happening to me. It just felt like I was going to die as I seemingly struggled with those breaths, with paramedics on standby. I asked them to take me back, but they refused. I remember one usher saying, "Ma'am, we cannot take you back in there. We do not know what the Holy Spirit is doing with you; He is still working with you and we do not know what's going to come out of your mouth."

At that point, I told them I didn't want to die and for someone to go in and tell them to pray for me. They asked me if I wanted water, and I nodded, and they brought it and gradually poured it into my mouth. Once my upper right body relaxed some, they decided to take me to the overflow room. On our way there, in the hallway, my body relaxed after about 20 to 25 minutes. I now went the complete opposite while in the hallway, flaccid! If you lifted my hand, it'd just drop as though I had no bone in me. One of the ushers commented, "Oh, she relaxed," but they noticed my body was sagging and realized they couldn't reach the overflow room, so they pulled a chair nearby and sat me there. After about four minutes, I was somewhat alert as I gazed up and saw a paramedic. I insisted that nothing was wrong with me and I didn't need her. She affirmed that she was there for emergency purposes, if need be. I calmed down for about ten minutes and then entered bouts of laughter. After ten more minutes, I went back into the hall. The service ended with us going through the fire tunnel. This was an experience that changed my life! It was God, so real! God deals with each of us uniquely. These were my experiences in my dealings with Him and so should not be used as a standard of doctrine. We must continue to chase after God and He will reveal Himself to us in any way He chooses.

Chapter 19
I Am Insatiable!

"The key to Christian living is a thirst and hunger for God. And one of the main reasons people do not understand or experience the sovereignty of grace and the way it works through the awakening of sovereign joy is that their hunger and thirst for God is so small."

-John Piper

After this incident my hunger for all things Kingdom was insatiable. This freezing experience would continue to happen at church every once in a while, sometimes during worship or just randomly. I'd often try to hide it although those close to me knew and would move in even closer to help hide the freeze. I'd be clapping my hands and they would just stay frozen, depending at what point of the clapping I was at, apart or together. I began to study more on the presence of God and dig deeper. I bought books of people who were into the presence and glory of God. I launched studies on how to hear God's voice. One time I remember doing a personal fast and I was reading a book on Kathryn Kuhlman. One fateful day as I was reading, I decided to take a break, and just spend some time in prayer and worship.

My husband was asleep downstairs as he'd worked overnight. I had some worship songs playing softly in the background and I began to raise my voice as I worshiped the Lord. Suddenly, I smelled something in the air and it really did smell like some good chicken tomato stew. I wondered to myself, *Why of all times, only when I'm fasting, does my husband decide to go into the kitchen?* I wasn't too happy about that because this was a no-food-fast. When I was done praying I decided to go downstairs so I could call him out on it. When I got downstairs, my husband was fast asleep and no one was in the kitchen. I got so confused. I texted Pastor Joshua, telling him about the weird occurrence. He asked me what book I was reading and I told him it was a book on Katherine Kuhlman and the Holy Spirit. He told me that was it! I was like, "what?" He said I can't read a book and not expect manifestations. He explained that it was the fragrance of the Holy Spirit. I was overwhelmed because the entire atmosphere in there smelled so good, I didn't even know how to describe it. So good!

Based on this experience, I then began to thirst for much more of God and sincerely wanted more encounters with Him. I began reading books on how to hear the voice of God and also to cultivate the supernatural dimension of Him. I immersed myself in many books and I read my Bible as well. The more I thirsted and shared the word of God, whether on social media or the local cell group I led, the hungrier I became. In January 2018, we were doing a 30-day corporate church fast. I had done up to a 21 day no-food-fast, water only, the year before, but this time around I felt the leading to do a 30 day no-food-fast, juice only. It was tough, plus my sister got married and graduated in the middle of my fast. I honestly didn't want to break my fast so I explained my situation to her. She understood so I still attended the wedding and God gave me the grace to complete the fast.

Please note that when I talk of setting time aside to fast extensively it didn't happen overnight. Fasting was never something I grew up doing. I learned about this at church. It all started with a day of fasting until 6 p.m., then went to three days until 6 p.m., then one week until 6 p.m., then 24 hours water-only-fast, three days water-only, seven days water-only, 14 days etc. and as I pressed into the things of God, I just went by the leading of the Holy Spirit. So all this happened over a year or two. Give yourself time if you are considering doing a fast. What I'd tell you is that no fast ever leaves you the same. Sometimes I had a prayer list with my specific desires as I embarked on the fast.

At some point I had a burden in my heart to gather a few people to just soak ourselves in worship every once in a while. I talked to the pastor about it and he gave me the go ahead. We dubbed it the Upper Room, and randomly scheduled our meetings, gathering at 10.30 p.m. and soaking ourselves in praise, worship and prayers until about 3.30 a.m. We didn't know precisely how each meeting would go, since we just yielded to the Holy Spirit, but we were always blessed.

Chapter 20
Prophecies, Heavenly Glitter, and Fellowship

"And it shall come to pass afterward
That I will pour out My Spirit on all flesh;
Your sons and your daughters shall prophesy,
Your old men shall dream dreams,
Your young men shall see visions."

-Joel 2:28,

At these meetings, something strange began to happen to me. I just felt the urge to say something, almost like someone feeling like vomiting and you just go, uncontrollably. It almost was like words were being forced out of my mouth. My mouth would just open and I began to express some words, sometimes general and other times specific words as I'd call the person's name. Over time I began to realize this was a prophecy. I know I always prayed to God to give me the gift of word of knowledge but never prophecy.

Word of knowledge is a supernatural revelation by the Holy Spirit on past or present situations, usually pointing to what God intends to do whereas prophecy is revealing the mind of God through man under the inspiration of the Holy Spirit. In any case, I decided to flow with it as there's truly a purpose for everything. Some words were confirmed by the individuals and others we didn't understand, so we decided to write them down and just save them for later. Some words were indeed confirmed later.

As we continued these meetings, something strange happened again. I began to speak in other languages. Sometimes tribal languages that could be interpreted by the individuals and other languages we didn't understand. Sometimes I'd pick up people's names in the spirit and just pray for them, whether we knew them or not. Other times I'd sense the presence of angels in the room and some would even see them. These experiences just made God more real to me. We'd continue to gather and pray, particularly when we had special programs at the Church.

I began to have a burden for women who either struggled to conceive or had complications in pregnancy. Some would call me to pray for them or others that I, or they, were aware of. I just prayed. There were many times when I prayed for these people that I'd starting crying profusely as though there was a weight on my shoulders. It was almost like their burdens were put on me. Glory to God, most have conceived and delivered children. Sometimes when we were praying for a particular sick person at church I would break down into tears. When I asked the pastor about such a feeling he explained I was driven by compassion to intercede for them.

As a result, my overall experiences at these Christian conferences, as well as church, led me to seek after the glory of God. I bought a bunch of books on the glory, many of which were authored by Ruth Heflin and I came to desire what I read through the pages of those books. I just wanted more of God and wanted Him to reveal Himself to me in supernatural ways. Even if He never blessed me with another child, I wanted to believe He was real.

At some point, I started to notice glitter on my hands, and sometimes on the pages of the books I was reading, including my Bible. I wasn't totally shocked because I had read about it in those books. They called it 'gold dust' or 'golden glory'. If someone else had told me about it, I would have said it was fake, but this was happening to me! I could not have fooled myself. My palms were filled with glitter. I began to take pictures and videos of it, so I could save it because I knew at some point the experience would stop. In the beginning I kept it to myself until I felt led to let the pastor know. He acknowledged it as signs and wonders but never did make a big deal about it. I never knew when it came or if I had to do something about it. I mentioned it to one of my sisters and she asked me to pray for someone when it happened.

One time, I visited a friend at her office and she said she wanted it. I said a very short prayer and left. She later called me saying her table, books and other things in the office were filled with glitter. From then on, she, too, started seeing it every now and then.

After sometime, I decided to show my son as well. He, too, began to see it every now and then, and he'd run up to me and say, "Momma, I have heavenly glitter!" I'd smile and just tell him it was a sign reminding us of God's presence. My sister-in-law visited and desired it. At one of our prayer sessions, amidst other things, I asked God to also reveal himself in a unique way to her with that sign and wonder. Lo and behold, a few days later her hands were also covered in gold dust! For me, this continued just about every Sunday after service on my drive home from church. On the Sunday evenings that I worked nothing would show up while at work; but as soon as I stepped into my car, it started and continued spreading on my hands until I got home, and throughout the night into the morning. I do still get my hands covered with the glitter just about every Sunday.

Since it happened to other people, including my pastor, I was convinced I wasn't crazy and it had to be God. I'd learned that signs and wonders are great, but we cannot get carried away by these, and begin to worship them which will cause us to miss God in seeking His signs. I'm so glad I also had a pastor who could guide me through this season, and told me to stick to the Word of God. Some people focus so strongly on things like this that they begin to chase it and not God. Signs and wonders point us to the Father, and will come and go, but His Word forever remains.

Chapter 21
Living Through the Pain

"When our days become dreary with low hovering clouds of despair, and when our nights become darker than a thousand midnights, let us remember that there is a creative force in this universe, working to pull down the gigantic mountains of evil, a power that is able to make a way out of no way and transform dark yesterdays into bright tomorrows."

-Dr. Martin Luther King Jr.

After Eliana passed, it was tough! I still asked God some questions that I couldn't answer, and I seemingly didn't get any answers from Him. It seemed like He broke His promise, because I knew too well what Nahum 1:9 says: "Affliction won't rise a second time," but after all my trusting God, it did! Didn't it? When you go through grief, you can choose to wallow in it or look for ways to rise above it. Things may never be the same again but you can move forward and find a new norm.

We rearranged our bedroom and gave away a lot of her stuff just because I didn't want sad memories lurking around me when I was trying to move on in a positive manner. We found our new norm and that was how we thrived. I'd cry when her brother, Jesse, would come telling me he misses her and he'd ask me difficult questions. I'd tell him she's in Heaven with the angels and having fun with all the other kids. I asked God to comfort Jesse for us.

One time during prayers at church, Jesse interrupted me and told me he saw her in a vision; he described her saying she looked so pretty. Another time, we were driving home from church and he looked up in the sky and said he witnessed her again. I just thanked God for the little assurances. I hate pity parties, because they leave me in a worse state of mind than I was in before. I decided to be strong and sort of avoid people who may, consciously or unconsciously, put me in that position.

In addition, it was hard living around people who were insensitive. I remember someone calling me and, in a bid to console me, telling me not to cry. In this person's words, "Why are you crying? Wipe your tears, was that even a baby? Let her go back to where she came from. Stop crying." Maybe to this person that was a way of consoling me, but it was like I was pierced with an arrow straight through my heart and the bleeding started all over again. I went into my closet and poured out my eyes. *Why? Why? Why do I have to go through this?*

One time we were visiting some friends and a casual conversation was taking place amongst the group. I can't quite remember how the conversation started. All I recall was one of our friends saying, "Anyone who has one child does so by choice." Of course this phrase was ignorantly expressed. It was almost like I had a built-in sensor that responded to stuff like that. I think I subtly spoke up, saying, "Not necessarily." I could almost immediately feel the pain of the many women who are struggling with childbearing.

One other time, my siblings and I were chatting in our family group on Whatsapp, and I remember one of them ignorantly conveying something like, "God has a way of doing things. The only boy in the family is the only one who has girls, and everyone else only has boys." Technically, that was true; however, I started crying because it made me feel like my girls didn't count because they'd passed on to Heaven. In my mind, I carried these babies and gave birth to them and lived with them. The fact that they weren't able to speak didn't discount the statistics of me carrying and birthing girls. Of course no one will understand where I was coming from so I let it drop and didn't continue in the conversation. When you haven't walked a mile in a person's shoes it's hard to know the areas that pinch.

Other times, I heard testimonies of God coming through for X, Y, Z people at church, and I wondered when my turn would come. I'd listen about the goodness of God… of children who were sick or even at the point of dying, and they were prayed for and the Lord came through. I'd be happy for them, but then that sent shivers down my spine and the emotional roller coaster expedited again. Sometimes tears welled up in my eyes as I sat in the service, and other times they'll just flow freely. On my way home, I'd cry and cry.

In 2016, the then Women's President at church was stepping down and the pastor urged me to take the position. This was a position I absolutely didn't want, besides being in the limelight. The pastor told me that it was going to be temporary until they found someone, so I agreed. Most people don't realize the behind the scenes work that involves such a position. I'd made up my mind to celebrate with other people regardless of how I felt, because it was no fault of theirs. I wasn't going to strip them of their joyful moments just because I faced some challenges. Only when I celebrated with them, would my own breakthrough evolve. The church was so blessed as we had several baby showers and over the years, I attended the ones I could and obviously took gifts to the expectant moms. When the babies arrived, I'd visit them in the hospital or send some representatives. Every time I walked into the hospital and held a baby, though I rejoiced I couldn't help but have those thoughts run through my mind. *When Lord?*

The babies would later be brought to church for dedication. Friends and family would dance to the altar to celebrate with the family. I happily followed along and as I stood there, imagining myself by the altar with my own baby, the enemy would flash thoughts saying it can't be me. I'd rebuke it and continue worshiping. I remember one such dedication, when the pastor was praying, I broke down crying as I pictured myself standing there.

The truth was there were some moments when my thoughts got the best of me. Why was it that while some women wanted babies so badly, others were trying to get rid of them? Why did God even bless them in the first place? Some lived a life of purity before they got married, and others lived recklessly; and as soon as they got married, they got pregnant and the babies started coming. Some who didn't go to church, nor do they even believe in God, would get pregnant by kissing! *So why me God?* I preserved myself for my future husband, I was obedient to my parents, I didn't have boyfriends all over the place, I did my best to serve God, so why me? I never did obtain any concrete answers.

I've heard people say if you aren't facing any challenges in life, then you and the enemy may very well be headed in the same direction? Was that supposed to make me feel better? I don't know, but I knew it was all a little too much for me. Could God take some of the pain away? As I write this, I now understand that it simply unveils another dimension of God's mercies to humankind. He isn't a tit-for-tat God!

Like I said earlier, one of the things that kept me going was when I redirected people to a God that offers hope to his children. I was leading a cell group in my home through those years, and I didn't stop just because I was facing my own challenges. The work of God doesn't come to a standstill because we're hurting. Whatever thing you want in life, be sure to give it away. You are scattering your seed all over, and in due time you will reap a harvest. God will give you the grace to offer hope to others. The more I offered hope to other people, the lighter I felt. We'd go out for door-to-door evangelism or in shopping centers, sometimes early Saturday mornings and other times in the evenings, ministering about the love of God to people. I remember this one lady whose house a couple of us stopped by; she let us in. We talked about Jesus, and decided to pray with her. It wasn't a long prayer. We may have sung one worship song, and the glory fell. I started to pray for her and may have mentioned something the Lord just laid on my heart for her. She cried profusely; we knew she was under the power of God. She thanked us and we left. I was so happy that we offered hope to that lady who said she was giving up. God had sent us there. Quite a few times the pastor would let me minister during our midweek services at church. I'd prepare on whatever the Lord laid on my heart. I remember so vividly one message the Lord asked me to minister on that I titled "Standing Tall in Your Wilderness." I laughed when I prepared the message, because God spoke to me through the message before He let me take it to others.

Chapter 22
Heart Ache

"When peace, like a river, attendeth my way,
When sorrows like sea billows roll;
Whatever my lot, Thou hast taught me to say,
It is well, it is well with my soul."

-Horatio Spafford

One day when I got back home from church in 2016, I had an impression to just write baby names and print a picture of a baby in the womb. I taped that picture behind my clothes in the closet where I'd pray every night, decreeing and declaring what I wanted. I'd look at that picture when I was done praying, so I could have an image in my mind. I'd stand on scriptures like:

Psalm 127:3

> *"Behold, children are a heritage from the LORD,*
> *The fruit of the womb is a reward."*

Exodus 23:26

> *"No one shall suffer miscarriage or be barren in your land; I will*
> *fulfill the number of your days."*

Psalm 89:34

"My covenant I will not break,
Nor alter the word that has gone out of My lips."

Psalm 118:17

"I shall not die, but live,
And declare the works of the Lord."

Sometimes I'd write them on flash cards and read them out loud every morning. I'd call out the nations I'd birth from the Heavens.

We didn't go into trying to conceive right after Eliana passed because I didn't want her to be a fleeting wind and us to sort of get a consolation baby, so we waited for about a year before we started trying to conceive. Getting pregnant had never been an issue for me, so once I decided to take out my IUD, Intrauterine Device, like I've always done in the past, I knew it'd just happen! After all, this would be the 4th pregnancy. We started trying and I noticed it didn't seem to happen as quickly as I thought. After about nine months I decided to set up an appointment with my OB-GYN to see if I could possibly take something to speed up the process. When I got there he came in to talk to me. He asked how long we'd been trying and I told him, and he said to keep trying and if it went past a year, to come back then. I bought a box of ovulation strips and pregnancy tests, tracked my temperatures with a basal thermometer, and we continued trying and went past a year and nothing happened.

Again, I returned to him. He told me we might be dealing with secondary infertility and was going to send us to Oklahoma University— OU— Hospital to start off with some tests and so on. This was a great doctor whom I had, and still have a good relationship with, but then I recalled so vividly his words: "I don't know, Carine, your uterus just cannot carry babies. You guys can look into adoption or surrogacy out of Texas, you know." There's absolutely nothing wrong with adoption as there are many kids out there looking for loving homes. Some parents have adopted and that actually turned out to be the best decision for both parties. However, that wasn't my plan and it felt like he had stabbed me.

I left the office crying, got home, and continued crying. It felt like one of those "Can anything good come out of Nazareth?" moments. I was written off. I may have mentioned to my husband what he said about secondary infertility, but not the adoption part. I decided I wasn't going to go to OU Hospital either. God had blessed me with one living child and if that was it, then fine and dandy.

Imagine going month after month looking forward to not seeing your period and yet it shows up each time. Some months, I'll even check 24 days out just to see if I'd get two solid lines. One time my period was delayed roughly 35 days, and just when I was about to get excited thinking a urine test would confirm it the period made a surprise entrance!

Early in 2017, I did get a positive test! How excited I was! I checked twice again, and it was positive. I immediately set up an appointment with the doctor. The appointment was about a month out and I couldn't wait. At seven weeks, I scheduled an appointment with a local ultrasound place in Edmond; I went in to see if there was indeed a baby in there. Yep, there was a gestational sac and a heartbeat. My doctor had earlier put me on Progesterone capsules to help with my irregular cycle and to continue taking until 10 weeks if I happened to get pregnant.

I attended a King Jesus Ministry conference in Florida, June 2017. I was about eight weeks pregnant at the time. I attended the conference and had a blast. While there, I felt the Lord leading me to sow a seed into that ministry. After all, I was pregnant and felt like I needed to seal the deal. It's vital to understand that you absolutely CANNOT buy a miracle from God but you can sow a seed and declare and decree what you want, as in commissioning it. I won't tell you how much, but that was one of the biggest financial seeds I've ever sowed until this date. The conference was great. I even celebrated my birthday while there.

Upon returning to Oklahoma, I had my 10-week appointment with my doctor. I visited on a Wednesday, and he congratulated me on the pregnancy. We proceeded to do the vaginal ultrasound. He saw the gestational sac. Yay! As he twisted the probe around, I noted how his facial expressions changed. I didn't understand what was happening. In my head, I decided to stay calm, and a few minutes later, he says, "Sorry, Carine. I'm so sorry, we can't find the heartbeat." I was shocked! I asked him what he meant. He said there wasn't a heartbeat and that it indicated that the baby actually stopped growing about week 8 or 9, somewhere in between. He alleged it pretty much was a missed miscarriage. I managed to keep a straight face, thanked him and walked out. I got into my car and bawled and bawled and bawled. My heart was aching;. I wondered when it all happened. *Did it happen before I went into the conference or at the conference, and I carried a dead fetus worshiping and praising God all along?* I sent a text to my husband, saying they couldn't find a heartbeat; I didn't even know how to tell him.

The doctor basically advised that I could either let nature take its course and it'll just come out or I could do a D&C. He said it was also okay to repeat the ultrasound. I scheduled an appointment with the Nurse Practitioner a couple of days later. I informed the pastor about it and he asked me to come for prayers. He gave me some anointing oil, and we agreed and asked God to intervene. I went in two days later, but there was still no heartbeat. I just couldn't imagine myself going to work knowing I carried a dead fetus in me. I couldn't bear the pain and thought of that so I elected for the D&C. My doctor wasn't going to be around since July 4th was around the corner, and I needed it done ASAP. We scheduled it and he had his partner do the procedure in June 2017, I believe. I went in, and all went well. I spent a night at the hospital and was discharged the next day.

Consequently, I emailed my scheduler at work and told her I needed a couple of days off, which she did give me. I cried and continued asking many questions that just didn't have any answers. My husband was there by my side, but I know he was devastated as well. I resumed work and life went back to normal. I remember one of my friends calling me and telling me about her pregnancy and I was happy for her and I imagined we were due about the same time. Well, my story had changed. When she had her baby, and even up to the dedication, I remember thinking mine would have been here, too. I gave myself a few months to heal and we continued trying.

My son Jesse would sometimes come up to me and tell me, "Momma, I really want a little brother." I asked him why not a sister, and he'd say he already had sisters and now it was time for a brother. I'd tell him to ask God for one. I'd go into my closet and cry, and inform God this kid wants a brother and I don't have one to give him, so please Lord hear His cry. Jesse would say this quite a few times and my response would always be the same; "Ask God."

After we tried for about a year, I told myself I was done. God had blessed me with one. Some don't have any, so this is life and I'm going to be happy and live with it. Victor and I were having a random conversation one day and when I said I'd hung my boots up he wasn't too happy about that. We sort of had a heated conversation with him asking me why it was entirely my decision, and not consulting him about it. I told him I wasn't dealing with it all again.

With my husband unhappy, I decided to sort of get a second opinion as far as the secondary infertility issue. The following year, with insurance changing, I decided to go see another OB-GYN. I scheduled an appointment, went in and simply told him what my issue was. He reviewed my history and told me if I conceived, the outcome would most likely not be good. He told me as a doctor, he had to tell me the truth, and so wouldn't even recommend I get pregnant. He said He believed in miracles, but laid out the reality I was facing. He asserted the first step was for them to see if I was ovulating at all. I was scheduled to come back and get my blood drawn a certain number of days after my period started the following month. I came in at that time and the blood was drawn. They called me with the results the following week and said my hormones were okay and I actually did ovulate. I got back home and told my husband the news.

Chapter 23
Man Proposes, But God Disposes

For I know the thoughts that I think toward you, says the Lord, thoughts of peace and not of evil, to give you a future and a hope.

-Jeremiah 29:11

I remember my pastor had told me to change my OB-GYN after I had had the miscarriage, but I had been reluctant. I believed my doctor knew me better than anyone else and I didn't want to go start all over with another person. I continued having my regular checkups with my current OB-GYN. Several months later, at one of the overnight Upper Room prayers, there was a prophetic word that came for me; the word was simply for me to do what the pastor had instructed me to do. The word was specifically for me; and once it came out, I knew exactly what it meant. The logic behind my pastor's reasoning was to turn a new leaf, and not be with one who every time I see him, I'm reminded of history.

The next day following the prayers, I told the Lord that I'd heard and would change OB-GYNs. I began searching and decided I was going to stick to the lady who did my D&C a year prior. After all, she was a nice lady. It was a hassle switching doctors since they didn't even want to transfer me because they were both in the same office. I explained to the staff that I had no problems with the former doctor, but just needed a change; they finally got me on her schedule.

I went in for my first appointment and we did general stuff, including a pap smear, I believe. I told her about some stomach pain issues and the irregular periods I sometimes had. I informed her that we had been trying to conceive for close to two years and the other doctor referred us to OU, but I think I'm happy with one child and don't want to open up a whole new chapter. She said she understood very well. She decided to schedule me for an ultrasound, so we could see where the pain was coming from and just look at my uterus. Once she got the results of the ultrasound, I was scheduled for another appointment. When I went in, she explained to me that they'd seen a couple of fibroids and cysts that may be causing that stomach pain. She said a fibroid was also blocking my endometrium and that may be what was preventing me from getting pregnant. She revealed we could schedule surgery and try to have it taken out, and we could try to conceive again, but it was no guarantee. I was scheduled three months ahead, for surgery September 4, 2019 at 12:45 p.m. In my mind, I said I was going to have the surgery and give this one last shot. I planned on trying a few times; and if nothing happened, I could tell my husband, at least we tried and permanently hang my boots up… even if it came with mixed feelings.

I continued my activities as normal. There was a Heaven Come conference organized by Bethel music in Dallas starting Thursday, August 29, 2019. I'd planned to go for that conference and so I did. I had my pre-op appointment on Wednesday August 28th at 10:15 a.m. At the pre-op, they just gave me a rundown of what kind of surgery I was going in for, signed some consent forms here and there, gave me my pre-op medications and all instructions they'd give you before surgery. Next day, I left for Dallas. I took along with me my sanitary pads, since I logged my periods and it was supposed to begin the day I left for Dallas. I don't like surprises, so I usually start putting those on a couple of days before the actual date, since it sometimes was off by a day or two anyways. I did put on my pads, changing them out throughout the entire conference, even though no bleeding had started yet.

It was an amazing time, as usual, at the conference. I met a few ladies from New Creation Church in Singapore and we bonded so well, and hung out through the entire conference. At some point in one of the sessions, some cases were called out, and we were asked to pray for the sick. Those who needed prayers stood up, and I told those who were surrounding me, to just pray for my womb. I said I needed God to give me a new womb. They prayed and prayed and one of the Singapore ladies prophesied over me.

Sunday morning, I left very early for Oklahoma so I could attend church in the city. Sunday evening, Miss Flo still hadn't shown up. Of course, pregnancy was the last thing on my mind, since it hadn't happened for two years. Plus, the surgery was supposed to help it happen; and if it happened after surgery, that would be great, too, so I could carry it through without any fibroids in the way.

On Monday, September 1st, the church's corporate 40 days of Fasting & Prayers started. I'd prayed for God to give me the grace to go through it. I woke up that morning fasting and I got tired of changing and wasting pads for almost one week and Miss Flo still wasn't here. I had one pregnancy test left in the cabinet, from a while back. I can't quite remember if it had expired or not. I pulled the test out, peed on the stick and two solid lines showed up. I was a little confused and thought it may be a defective stick. I quickly stepped out of the house and purchased two other tests, one digital and the other a pack of two regular ones. I came home, tested with two of them again. The digital one said pregnant, and I had two solid lines on the other one. I decided to save one test for the first morning urine the next day as I thought maybe it was late in the afternoon. The next morning, which was Labor Day, I did it and it was two solid lines again!

Based on these tests, I went to the living room and casually told my husband that I may be pregnant. He smiled, looked at me and told me to stop throwing jokes.

I said I was serious. I told him I'd taken about four tests that all said positive, but would have to call the doctor's office the next day and see if it is truly positive. I would also have to find out if there was any possibility I could go ahead with the surgery which was to take place a day later. After all, the pregnancy would have been still too early I thought to myself. On Wednesday, September 3rd, I called and told them I had a positive pregnancy test and they just told me upfront they'd have to cancel the surgery that was to happen the next day. They scheduled me for an eight-week OB appointment. Meanwhile I informed the pastor of what was going on, but didn't tell him I'd decided to continue with my fasting and prayers because he'd say no. All along I still went to the gym, continued my 5.30 a.m. prayers at home, and I decided to stop the fasting on day 21, but I continued going to church for the evening prayers. Somewhere in the back of my mind, I still was thinking Miss Flo was pulling one on me and she may show up. I was excited, but I was still trying to understand how it happened. It never happened when we were intimate almost every other day, so how did it happen when our intimacy had been sporadic? I couldn't even remember our last time. The harder I thought about it, the more confused I got so I just left it alone.

Isn't it funny how we pray for a blessing from God, trusting God to come through for us, yet when He does, we either fail to recognize or refuse to acknowledge it? We see that in Acts 12, when Peter was thrown into prison and the church gathered to earnestly pray for him. When their prayers were answered, Peter himself showed up at the door, but they were still astonished and thought it was his angel. When we pray, we must create an image in our minds and remain expectant.

In the process, I understood that when God Himself wants to do something, He will do it in such a way that absolutely no one else can claim to take the glory for it. This was definitely one of those situations. God did it, not because I fasted or prayed, but out of His mercies and to show His glory and faithfulness.

About six or so weeks into the pregnancy, I started spotting about daily or every other day. I panicked but prayed about it. My excitement now turned into cautious excitement. I told Victor about the bleeding so he was aware and in the back of my mind I was preparing him for the worse. I also informed the pastor about it, so he prayed for me from time to time. He also gave me some communion and anointing oil as well. This continued into week seven and I wasn't able to sleep. I went to work one day and the bleeding was more than pantyliner bleeding as I had to change pantyliners. I decided to call the doctor's office, and they told me to just go to the ER because there wasn't anything they could do immediately from their end. After work, I contacted Victor and told him I was headed to the ER because the bleeding increased. I pretended to stay calm but I honestly had made up my mind for the worst that could happen.

Yes, I prayed. I told God, this child was put there by Him, not me. He gave the child this time without my knowledge for a reason, so let it either make it through or if not, if this is another miscarriage, let it just happen now and not let me carry this pregnancy for all to see and have to live with pain again. I went in and was wheeled into my room. The doctor came in and decided to do an ultrasound and a pelvic exam. I couldn't hear anything as it was on his lap top, so I was looking at his facial expressions. He quietly did his stuff as he examined. I just blurted out: "Is there a heartbeat?" and he said, "O yea, but we need to do the pelvic exam to see about the bleeding." He stepped out and returned a few minutes later to do the pelvic exam. He explained that it was a threatened miscarriage and that there was still some blood in there, so I should expect it to come out; it could be as long as a week, he didn't know.

Whew!! I walked out of there smiling again. I sent a text to Victor saying there was a heartbeat. Week eight, I went in for my actual appointment and by that time, the bleeding had stopped. My OB-GYN was happy for me and she stated, "Well, no more surgery for right now." Then I told her God must have had other plans.

Chapter 24
Trusting God and the Process

"Don't only trust God, but also trust the process He is taking you through."

-Carine Njoh

Week ten, I scheduled an appointment with a local ultrasound place in the city, so I could find out the sex of the baby. I went in and they said it was a boy! I was excited for Jesse especially, because that was his desire all along. I walked out thinking of what name to give him. I pulled up Google, trying to look for the Hebrew word for healing. Lo and behold, the first name that popped up in my mind was Josiah. I quickly looked up the meaning and it said, "Jehovah has healed."

When I got home, I immediately checked my dream book and the first page, dated on September 28, 2016, the Lord had instructed me to write down a couple of names and Josiah was the first. I panicked because I truly had forgotten. Then I remembered there was a personalized onesie I ordered about the same time with the name He had given me. I went and dug into my clothes drawers and I found that onesie with the receipt dated August 2016. I started crying and I thanked God for the name He had revealed years prior. All through the pregnancy, the Lord had been ministering to me that the baby would bring healing, not just to my family but to all who need healing in one way or another, as long as they opened themselves up. Yes-even those reading this book miles and miles away.

My subsequent OB appointments were scheduled monthly, and she also scheduled me to see a maternal-fetal specialist on a monthly basis as well. I remember my 12-week appointment with her and the nurse checking the heart beat using a Doppler. You may not understand, but I did feel good because it felt like it was a normal pregnancy. In the past they always had to do a full ultrasound, even at my regular OB-GYN's office. I went for my monthly appointments with the specialist and he knew my history as well as he'd seen me during the previous pregnancies. Every time the ultrasound tech came in and did their measurements and all, she'd mention about them monitoring the growth of some fibroids they'd seen. I always acted like I didn't know what she was talking about, but I knew exactly where they were as they did hurt sometimes. However, when they said that, it came in through one ear and I let it go right out through the other. I didn't want to focus on the fact that I had a fibroid and could harness negative energy from there.

Since I lacked an explanation as to why what was happening to me in the past kept occurring, the specialist also told me the chances of that occurring again were very high. He advised me to keep praying and just stay positive. Every time I went in there, he'd look and tell me everything looked okay and then reminded me to stay positive. He and my OB-GYN communicated, so as precautionary measures, they both agreed that I'd be admitted into the hospital once the baby was of viable age. That way, if anything were to happen, I'd be two minutes from the Operating Room, instead of being 10 minutes away.

Through this process, I've discovered that just because you heard from God concerning a situation, didn't mean that it would automatically happen. The enemy knows quite well what God's plan is for you, so he'll begin fighting as soon as that prophecy is released or when you hear from God. The enemy will want to prove to everyone around you, especially the faithful, that God doesn't exist; he'll jump at every opportunity to defend his stand. What better person to use than a spirit-filled, tongue speaking believer!

When we hear the Word we must contend for that spoken word to pass. I continued praying and just thanking God for each week. Some days I took communion and then anointed my belly. I began to call Josiah by name. I'd decree and declare what I wanted to see. Many believers trust God yet they doubt His process. I learned to not just trust God, but also trust the process He was taking me through. I didn't know what was in my future, but I was confident in the God of my future.

Genesis 2:7 tells us that God breathed his spirit into man and man became a living being. We don't like to admit it but life is more spiritual than physical. Man is a spirit being who has a soul and lives in a body. Everything that happens to us in the physical realm has already taken place in the spirit realm. It's left for us to be discerning and take care of business in the spiritual before it manifests in the physical. However, we've trained ourselves much more in the physical realm than we have in the spirit realm. In the physical realm, we can see a person cross the street or a person walk into a store and have a business transaction with another person. Such a reality is also present in the spirit realm; however, we don't train ourselves in that realm nor do we tap into it so we miss it. Others, like palm readers and mediums, get into it and wrongly use it. You and I have the same God-given ability that we can properly put into use for good, but we must train ourselves to be sensitive to the Spirit. It's important to also note that spirits, good or bad, cannot operate on their own without a body.

A covenant is a legally binding agreement between two parties. I strongly believe that if there are covenants that work in our favor, such as the Abrahamic covenant under which we claim blessings, then there also exists covenants under which people are cursed. Ungodly covenants ought to be broken and not rebuked. Many of us don't know the past of our parents or ancestors and so covenants made to any deity, good or bad, work for or against us. They are binding, even by virtue of relationships such as marriage. Being oblivious of an existing covenant does not make it disappear nor does it exempt you from the benefits or repercussions of it. We must therefore seek understanding, otherwise we perish for a lack of knowledge(Hosea 4:6).

Ephesians 6:12 "For we do not wrestle against flesh and blood, but against principalities, against powers, against the rulers of the darkness of this age, against spiritual hosts of wickedness in the heavenly places." We therefore are engaged in a spiritual and not physical fight. Anything that happens in the physical has already occurred in the spiritual, and many times we are still playing catch up. With all this knowledge, and to cover all my basis, I'd pray and break any ungodly covenants entered into by either of our ancestors, whether knowingly or unknowingly, especially coming from an African background. Sometimes, a covenant may also need a higher power to dissolve. I also prayed some prayers adapted from a *Prayer Mantle Book* by a Mountain of Fire and Miracle Ministry Pastor in Ireland that I came across several years ago. I further shared these prayers with ladies I prayed for, regarding the fruit of their wombs. Here are some excerpts below:

PRAYERS FOR PREGNANT WOMEN (MFMM)

MONDAY

1. My Father, I thank you for making me reproductive in life.
2. My Father, I thank you for disgracing barrenness in my life.
3. Blood of Jesus, mix with my blood and that of my baby.
4. Fire of God, possess me and the baby in my womb in the name of Jesus.
5. Lord, my baby shall not be aborted by dark powers.
6. My health will not be tampered with during this period of pregnancy.
7. I receive strength to carry my baby in my womb for nine months.
8. My baby will not become sick in the womb.
9. Jaundice will not attack my baby.
10. The formation of my baby shall be perfect.

TUESDAY

1. The baby in my womb, shall not be an abnormal baby.
2. The head of my baby will not carry any curse.
3. Any curse that operated in my life will not affect my baby.
4. My baby, you will not be paralyzed inside the womb.

5. Fire of God, possess my life and that of my baby.

6. My womb will not be too hot to accommodate my baby.

7. My baby will stay in the correct position in my womb.

8. The eyes of the baby will not go blind in the womb.

9. My enemies will not have access to the blood of my baby.

10. I immerse my baby and my womb in the pool of the blood of Jesus.

WEDNESDAY

1. My baby will not be deaf and dumb in my womb.

2. Witchcraft power will not locate my baby in my womb.

3. My baby, you will have enough food to eat in my womb.

4. My baby will drink the blood of Jesus and eat the fire of God.

5. My baby will not die in my womb.

6. My baby, you shall come out with your head first on the day of delivery.

7. I shall be congratulated on the day of delivery.

8. My baby shall be active in my womb.

9. All the parts of my baby will function very well.

10. The power of the grave shall not swallow my baby.

THURSDAY

1. My baby will not be possessed.
2. The head of my baby shall not be bewitched.
3. Holy ghost, possess the destiny of my baby.
4. My baby will receive extra power to overcome sickness in the womb.
5. My baby, you shall be the head and not the tail.
6. My baby, you shall be greater than your father.
7. Mortuary powers will not kill my baby.
8. Wicked arrows will not enter the head of my baby.
9. My joy shall increase on the day of my delivery.
10. My baby shall be great in life.

FRIDAY

1. My environment must cooperate with my pregnancy.
2. The blood of my baby shall not be contaminated.
3. The satanic eye will not monitor the growth of my baby in my womb.
4. O Lord, make my baby a child of promise.
5. O God, arise and destroy the enemies of my baby.

6. Fire that swallows fire, enter the life of my baby.
7. Let the angels in chariots of fire surround my baby.
8. You the star, the sun, and the moon, cooperate with my baby.
9. The destiny of my baby will not be turned.
10. I will not deliver a premature baby.

SATURDAY

1. Disease associated with the womb, my life is not your candidate.
2. Fire of deliverance and healing, enter my womb.
3. Any power chanting on my womb, die.
4. My womb shall not be the coffin of my baby.
5. Anointing safe delivery, fall upon me now.
6. Fire that brings victory, enter my womb.
7. I receive Hebrew woman anointing by fire.
8. I will not lose too much blood on the day of the delivery.
9. The eyes of my baby will not go blind.
10. The legs of my baby will not be paralyzed.

SUNDAY

1. My baby, receive fresh fire.
2. My prayers spoil the joy of my enemies in the name of Jesus.
3. My baby, you will not be delivered with sickness.

4.   Every fire of premature delivery burning in my life, die.

5.   Any power planning to steal my baby in the womb, die.

6.   Any power planning to steal my baby at birth, be paralyzed.

7.   Any power planning to exchange my baby, receive paralyses.

8.   Blood of Jesus, be my helper, on the day of my delivery.

9.   Planter of sickness in my womb and the life of my baby, die.

10.   Holy Spirit, be my divine surgeon on the day of delivery.

Chapter 25
Jehovah Has Healed!

"You have turned for me my mourning into dancing
You have put off my sackcloth and clothed me with gladness,
To the end that my glory may sing praise to You and not be silent.
O Lord my God, I will give thanks to You forever."

-Psalm 30:11-12,

One night at home, at about 3.30 a.m., I had a very bad dream and my husband, who was in the living room, heard me crying and sort of moaning in my sleep. He came to the bedroom to ask me if I was okay. I told him I was, but I'd had a bad dream. In the dream, the baby was pushing through my birth canal, obviously very prematurely, and I was trying to push his head back in. I cried and tried to make my way to the hospital. My sister and some other people were crying and saying, "No, it's too early; he can't come now," and I woke up panting. It was very scary. I knew I had to go into the place of prayer immediately and rebuke that dream. I went into my prayer closet and sent a text to one of my prayer warrior sisters and my pastor to intercede. I canceled whatever negative thing was trying to happen and began decreeing and declaring what I wanted to see. After about 30 minutes, I felt peace in my spirit so I went back to sleep. Compared to the previous pregnancies, this really was the only nightmare I had and I knew I'd taken care of that.

When I was about 26 weeks, I checked into the hospital and the plan was to deliver the baby at about 32 weeks. When I got to my room, I anointed the door post, spoke positive words into the atmosphere, and declared whatever evil spirit that might be there to pass over me, just like the death angel passed over the Egyptian door posts that were marked with blood. (Exodus 12:23) Every single day that went by was a blessing. I didn't even know how to pray again, and I just kept thanking God and asking Him to have mercy on me. My doctor, or her partner, would check on me daily. I had weekly ultrasounds from the Perinatal Center, to make sure all was in place. The entire team was wonderful. They gave me steroid shots the same day I checked in and sometime later a magnesium infusion all for the benefit of the baby in case he was to show up early. The nurse prepared an emergency C-section kit that was right there on the counter. The doctor informed the NICU staff and the 24-hour OB-GYNs at the hospital, and they had my name on the board. She told me they were well prepared in case the worst was to happen.

You know, what we feed will always grow. Our energy will always go towards what we choose to focus on. Some days were definitely fearful where I'd wonder what was going on in my tummy. Sometimes the baby moved too much and I'd want him to slow down; but if he slowed down too much, I'd worry if I didn't feel him move even for 30 minutes. I remember complaining to my doctor about him being too active, and she told me that was a good problem to have. If I felt the slightest pain, I'd fret if it was a rupture about to happen. I experienced these thoughts, but I'd make myself snap out of them very quickly as I didn't want to dwell on it and feed them. We may have negative thoughts every now and then, but it becomes a problem if we allow it to make its way to our hearts where we nurse it.

When I got to the hospital, I made up my mind to be positive at all times. No entertainment of negative news. I had the choice to be either moody and cry 'poor little me' or just be happy and enjoy the process. Of course, I chose the latter. I'd wake up every morning, turn all bright lights on, play gospel music, read uplifting books, listen to messages, watch *Candid Camera,* etc. I just had to be upbeat at all times. When people walked into the hospital, thinking they were coming to visit and sympathize with me, my attitude made them quickly change their minds.

About a week before the baby was born, Jesse came by my bedside and asked, "Momma, is the baby going to look like Eliana when he's born?" I understood exactly what he meant, but I wanted to make sure. I asked him what he meant and he asked if he was going to have all the tubes Eliana had. I then reminded him that Eliana had some complications, so that's why she had all those. I reassured him how I was checked into the hospital to prevent all those complications, and all our trust is in God, so the baby was going to be healthy like Jesse was.

My doctor scheduled delivery for March 4, 2020, and she said she wanted all hands-on deck. She had my former doctor, who delivered the girls, and another partner to help with the surgery. She also expected I'd have much blood loss and would need a transfusion so they were prepared. The night before my anxiety levels were off the roof. A team of about ten to fifteen people from church came by that night and prayed with me to ease my apprehension. Only the pastor knew the baby was going to be delivered the next day. On Wednesday, March 4, 2020, I woke up feeling a lot better. It seemed 5 p.m. was so far away. As they wheeled me into the Operating Room, my nerves got the best of me again. I started gagging a lot, even after I was given something for nausea and anxiety. Keep in mind, I'd never been awake during delivery and the thought of it rather scared me. I arrived there, and the anesthesiologist administered the epidural. Let's just say I'm glad there was no recording of me in there. My screams explained it all.

At 5:36 pm, Josiah *(Jehovah has healed)* **Asher** *(Blessed/Happy)* **Mborinwi** *(tribal-God's Anointing, God's grace, God's abundance of Blessings)* **Njoh was born, weighing 4 Ibs 2.7 oz, and 16.14 inches long.** It is one thing to have faith in God, for faith is the substance of things hope for, the evidence of things not seen, and

150

another to see that come into fruition, its tangibility. Tears of joy rolled down my cheeks when they brought Josiah to me. What I had seen with the eyes of my spirit for so many years, was finally in front of me! My husband was dealing with his own emotions while he tried to take pictures. Then one of the nurses took his phone and got a few pictures of us together. Most people in the Operating Room were from the team we'd dealt with in the past. The joy in the room was palpable. Later, my doctor recalled how she turned around, looked at the team and smiled. She told them that though they sometimes feel crappy at their jobs, moments like this make them love what they do. We were happy and so was everyone else. Since Jesse could not go into the NICU, his favorite nurse who'd taken care of him during his NICU days, went and got him to see his brother before he was taken into the NICU. Jesse was on Cloud 9! He kept saying His prayers were answered. The doctor said the surgery went quicker than she expected-25 minutes- and since I didn't lose much blood, no transfusion was needed. Glory to the Most High God!

Chapter 26
Choose Joy

"Participate joyfully in the sorrows of the world. We cannot cure the world of sorrows, but we can choose to live in joy."

- Joseph Campbell

Like I said earlier, I'm a very private person and really don't like putting any of my business out there. When I heard the Minister of the Gospel proclaim that our faith is personal, not private, with the help of the Holy Spirit, I decided to go all out in the book. I may have started writing this book in 2017 and paused along the line because I just knew my story wasn't complete. God doesn't write tragedies. Before I began, I prayed and asked the anointing of God to come upon me as I wrote. I didn't want it to just be any other book. Since God indeed asked me to write it, I yearned for it to be a book where the reader could experience hope, healing, and the presence of God. I hope it's doing just that. I didn't want you to come into this and leave the same way you came in. I wanted your strength to be renewed!

Without God, I don't know where I'd be. Through it all, I aimed to be happy. I knew I was a child of God, so I took solace in the fact that He has a better plan for me. I trusted God would work everything out for my good. The two bracelets I always wore had the scriptures Romans 8:28, "*And we know that all things work together for good to those who love God, to those who are called according to His purpose.*"

Jeremiah 29:11 "*For I know the thoughts that I think toward you, says the LORD, thoughts of peace and not of evil, to give you a future and a hope.*"

If you're going through some challenges right now, I want you to take a second and pause. Take a mental look around you, see what you have that others do not have. Do you see anything that is working for you that may not for others? Can you remember the last time God came through for you? Can you then say, "Lord forgive me for being ungrateful, Thank you Lord?" You see how the enemy distracts us? He turns your focus to that challenge, and makes you forget about the faithfulness of God, even when we've been unfaithful. He will want you to be so sucked up into the situation that you miss the message God is trying to communicate to you.

Don't focus on that challenge because what you focus on will grow and grow. In other words, you give it a life of its own. The enemy has a way of sucking us into throwing pity parties. He'll remind you of your predicament over and over, and even bring to your mind negative memories of people who are in better situations than you and are apparently having it good. This may even be people who don't pray or go to church. He'll paint them as successful in your eyes so you could think the worldly standard is the way to go. He wants you to believe the lie that you are the only one in the world with that challenge. He'll seek to make you feel sorry for yourself and then that keeps you in a depressed state. Understand that you are not the first to go through the challenge and you won't be the last either.

Depression is simply you having a conversation with your own thoughts. Don't get comfortable with that pattern because what we conform to is what remains. You must get uncomfortable or dissatisfied with it and desire a change. I'm by no means against medication. If you get into a depressive state, seek medical help, please. However, this, in my opinion, will only act as a band aid. While the medication can serve as a bridge, it's best to meditate on the Word of God day and night. Whatever situation you're dealing with, CHOOSE joy. If the enemy can succeed in stealing your joy then he has crippled you because a lack of it leads to despair which opens the door to depression. Cultivating joy should be a conscious effort as tough as it may be amidst turmoil.

Like my situations demonstrate, there will be times when you'll look around you and not find anything that should give you joy. Unlike happiness, joy isn't dependent on your surroundings. It's in such moments when Nehemiah 8:10 "…Do not sorrow, for the joy of the LORD is your strength." comes to life! Your strength will only be found in experiencing the joy of the

Lord. If you're facing some challenges I can't stress this enough— soak yourself in the Word.

Of course it takes time and sacrifice. Get into a deeper relationship with God. My trials made me realize how little of God I knew. The more time you spend with a friend, the more you know them and the more you gain their trust. If you spend time with God the better you will know Him. You come to that safe place where you just know you cannot doubt Him. You just trust that all is well. Like a mom clutches her baby to her chest and the baby can feel her heartbeat it's the same with us and God. You cannot feel His heartbeat from a distance. Go closer and lean into Him. Once you feel his heartbeat, you'll feel how big His love for you is regardless of the circumstances you face. Get into the secret place— the place of intimacy with the Father— and He'll share deep secrets with you. To access the depths of the Father we must first reach into our own depths, as cited in Psalms 42:7 "Deep calls unto deep."

Likewise, Paul tells us in Philippians 4:8 "Finally, brethren, whatever things are true, whatever things are noble, whatever things are just, whatever things are pure, whatever things are lovely, whatever things are of good report, if there is any virtue and if there is anything praiseworthy--meditate on these things." This therefore means if it's *not* true, not noble, not pure, not lovely… such as negative news or doctors' reports, we should *not* focus on it. You cannot focus on something and look away from it at the same time. If you focus on it you zoom in on it and bring it into perspective or reality.

So focusing on the negative will only lead to depression. If the doctor gives you or your loved one a negative report don't go to Google; instead, go to the Gospel. When I was told I had a uterine rupture, I remembered having learned about it at school and knew it was bad but I didn't remember any details. I made up my mind not to look it up because I didn't need to know any more than that. I didn't need to get into any statistics and start thinking I was doomed for life. I only looked it up once, when I started writing this book. When our mind tries to wander away from the Word we must pull it back. Do whatever it takes to flood your mind with positive things even if it means avoiding negative people. I pulled back from a lot of things and people because they just weren't helping me. I wasn't trying to be mean in any way, nor were they, but I needed to take care of myself at the time in order to avoid being drained. Some will understand but others never will. Just take care of you.

Many don't understand that God created marriage solely for the purpose of companionship, and children are a byproduct of that marriage. In the African culture, especially when one gets married, there's mounting pressure for children to start coming forth. If one year goes by and they see nothing, they start watching you; then year two and on. If no child seems to be coming forth, they begin asking you questions. Even if you have one, in their minds, you're supposed to have another one and they keep watching. I want to caution everyone reading this to please be sensitive when dealing with women who are expecting children. You don't know the behind the scenes details of everyone's story, so the most you can do is simply show love. Unless they're open about it, don't ask them any questions.

If you care much for them pray for them in your prayer closet. Give them random hugs, just because. People don't have their challenges written in caps on their foreheads. You may ask a woman when she's getting pregnant or why she doesn't have children yet, and guess what? That just may be the day she suffered a miscarriage; perhaps she just saw her period— that she's not been looking forward to— or she completed her 9th failed IVF treatment. She might possibly have been diagnosed with fibroids, Polycystic ovary syndrome-PCOS- or even endometriosis. C333hoose empathy. Maybe she just buried a child, had a hysterectomy, or another serious struggle. She may likely smile and merely say "soon", yet she probably goes back into her closet and cries. Don't be the reason any of these women shed tears.

A lady who had been trusting God for the fruit of her womb for so many years actually shared her story with me. Over a period of eight or so years, she's had a few miscarriages and failed IVF treatments. One day she attended an occasion and was holding her friend's baby. Then another lady walked by her and told her not to just hold her friend's baby but to make sure she has her own. The lady revealed how she responded that God would bless her with her own but she ultimately went home crying. Long story short, she's now blessed with two kids today. If there was a marketplace where babies were purchased we'd all go there, so please be sensitive to other people's challenges. There is also no need to *repeatedly* make statements like "God will also bless you with yours" only when you both are around a newborn. We all sincerely know that, so just keep praying privately.

If you're trusting God for the fruit of the womb I encourage you to celebrate with other women who are celebrating. Initially, it may seem hard but tell God you sincerely want to share in the other person's joy. He will give you the grace. Bless them with gifts when you can. Pray for their children. Spend time in prayer for other women who may be in the same, or an even worse situation than you are currently. Sometimes pregnant women may not know how to announce their pregnancies to you or how to talk to you because they don't know how it'll make you feel. Make them comfortable by talking about and sharing in their joys. All this will sow good seeds and in due time, you'll reap your harvest!

I remember a minister saying, "Mary was ridiculed for what she carried-an illegitimate child. It is important that you are mocked for what you carry." When you stand in faith trusting God for anything get ready also to be mocked. They say faith is also spelled RISK, because that's just what it is. You believe adamantly, even when everything around you is at odds with what you intended.

Chapter 27
The Goodness of God

"If God has done what you think he should do, trust him. If God doesn't do what you think he should do, trust him. If you pray and believe God for a miracle and he does it grant it, trust him. If your worst nightmare comes true, believe he is sovereign. Believe he is good."

-Craig Groeschel

Don't try to escape your pain. Embrace it and walk in it, because it's only at this point that you'll be able to walk in your purpose. Your tears aren't wasted; they are a road map or trail to your calling. I recently discovered a post that said something like, "One day you will tell your story of how you've overcome what you're going through now, and it will become part of someone else's survival guide." This is so true and the reason I decided to write this book. I want people to know that as long as we live, there are challenges we all will face, but they aren't the end of the world. Recognize the challenges you go through as seasons. We go through seasons of summer, fall, winter and spring. None of them is permanent. Sometimes, the summers may be too hot, but you know Fall will come around at some point.

You don't shut yourself up at home waiting for Fall to come around. Likewise, a season in your life may not be too pleasant, but you have to keep moving. You make the best of it. The Holy Spirit is a very present help in times of trouble, so we call upon Him to help us in such seasons. We may not always understand what God is doing but it is important we walk in obedience, as our victory is also tied to it.

In such seasons God may sometimes seem distant, but He is right there. I realized that He speaks, even in silence, only if you'd listen. Mark Batterson says "silence is anything but passive waiting. It's proactive listening." God promises us that He will never leave us nor forsake us. God doesn't author tragedies. If you just continue to hang on, focus on Him as you maintain your joy. Ecclesiastes 3:11 reminds us that He has made everything beautiful in *its* time. That, therefore, means there's *a* time for the beauty of anything to come out so simply wait for it. When you can't pray just go into a room and play some instrumental soaking music and bask in His presence. If you can speak in tongues, pray in tongues too. Sing in tongues. You'll come out refreshed. When all is said and done, you'll testify! However, keep in mind that it won't be because you prayed, fasted, sowed or worshiped enough. In essence it'll all be because of the grace of God!

On the other hand, what if? Just what if God doesn't answer our prayers like we want Him to? His Word still holds true. It is never nullified just because you did not get what you trusted Him for. We must come to that place where we can boldly say, "God, even if you didn't bless me at all, I will still serve you." Don't ever define the goodness of God based on, nor is it directly proportional to, your prevailing circumstances. The Bible tells us He is good, and so we must believe it, and that settles it! The Psalmist also tells us to taste and see that the Lord is good. Seeing here is experiencing the goodness of God. Divine encounters will also lead you into experiencing His goodness, so desire them. Imagine you taste honey and someone else comes to convince you on how bitter honey is. You'd laugh at them. Likewise, when you have truly tasted of the goodness of God you know He is good and no one can convince you otherwise, not even your circumstances. I've always understood faith as trusting and believing God until you get the desired outcome. When we don't get that desired outcome we often think we didn't have faith. People try to weigh in on why things turn out otherwise and sometimes imply that you didn't, or don't, have enough faith. It's a lot easier for people to talk about faith, until shit hits the fan on their end and they have to actually walk in it.

I believe faith is total trust and dependence on God in the face of challenging circumstances, and the ability to continue to trust God even when one doesn't get the desired outcome. That, to me, is a huge testament of one's faith.

1 Thessalonians 5:18 reminds us how *"in everything give thanks; for this is the will of God in Christ Jesus for you."* That verse tells us to give Him thanks in EVERYTHING. It doesn't say some things. Everything. So why not just keep thanking Him? That's His will for us; that we thank Him at all times. If it helps, look around and thank Him for what you think is working instead of focusing on what's not. Regardless, God remains God and He is good.

Before the fall of man, we were in a state of El Dorado-fabulous wealth and opportunity- like my pastor would say. After the fall of man, sin entered the world. Sickness, disease, hate, murder, etc., came in. The coming of Jesus Christ was to redeem us from sin and give us an opportunity to not suffer from the consequences of that sin— to sort of create immunity to that. However, you have to appropriate it. It won't just fall on your laps.

Accepting Jesus Christ as your Lord and Savior is the first step. If you haven't already accepted Jesus as your personal Lord and Savior, may I invite you to do so. Say out loud this prayer: 'Lord Jesus, I come to you as a sinner and I ask you to forgive me of all my sin. I believe you died and rose again from the dead so that I may be saved. I surrender myself to you, giving you my heart and my life and to follow you from this day on. Amen.' Now you've earned the right to appropriate all that Jesus paid the price for.

According to 2 Timothy 3:16-17, all scripture is inspired by God. The only good news that will remain constant in this world is the Word of God. The Bible is the Good News and if you always want good news, you must always fall back to it. As long as you live you'll encounter challenges in life. The only way to avoid those is to die. God has given us a way of escape in the ability to rise above those challenges and be in control of them, so they don't swallow you up, which again, is in His Word. The problem with most people is they're filled with a false sense of pride which prevents their acceptance of the fact that they can be dependent on something unseen to give them peace.

Let's take a look at Matthew 14:22-33

22 Immediately Jesus made His disciples get into the boat and go before Him to the other side, while He sent the multitudes away. 23 And when He had sent the multitudes away, He went up on the mountain by Himself to pray. Now when evening came, He was alone there. 24 But the boat was now in the middle of the sea, tossed by the waves, for the wind was contrary.

25 Now in the fourth watch of the night Jesus went to them, walking on the sea. 26 And when the disciples saw Him walking on the sea, they were troubled, saying, "It is a ghost!" And they cried out for fear.

27 But immediately Jesus spoke to them, saying, "Be of good cheer! It is I; do not be afraid."

28 And Peter answered Him and said, "Lord, if it is You, command me to come to You on the water."

29 So He said, "Come." And when Peter had come down out of the boat, he walked on the water to go to Jesus. 30 But when he saw that the wind was boisterous, he was afraid; and beginning to sink he cried out, saying, "Lord, save me!"

31 And immediately Jesus stretched out His hand and caught him, and said to him, "O you of little faith, why did you doubt?" 32 And when they got into the boat, the wind ceased.

33 Then those who were in the boat came and worshiped Him, saying, "Truly You are the Son of God."

In this story, we first notice that when Jesus came from the place of prayer, there was a storm waiting for Him. That too will happen to us. You may be in a period of fasting and prayers, and when you are done it may seem like all hell broke loose. It is important that we pray at all times to prepare us for what lies ahead. Just like Jesus was strengthened in the place of prayer for His own storms, your place of prayer will also strengthen and equip you for what you may face ahead.

Secondly, the disciples were troubled when they saw Jesus walk on water. Peter, on the other hand, asked Jesus to bid him come. Peter in the midst of the storm, began to walk on water as He focused on Jesus. Notice that while He walked on water, the winds were still present. Peace is therefore not the absence of trouble. Peace is simply the ability to remain calm in the midst of turmoil due to your focus on the One who is in charge. We are told Peter began to sink when He saw the boisterous winds. You can't look to your challenge and Jesus at the same time. You can either look to Jesus and thrive or look at the challenge and sink.

There is nothing new under the sun. When we go through the Bible, we see accounts of people who trusted in God and thrived in challenging times. We can do the same. Paul looked up to God during his time in prison. He wrote most of the New Testament you and I read today, from his prison cell. He had the option of bowing his head down and crying every day asking God when this will be over with. Joseph was disliked and betrayed by his brothers, plotted against by Potiphar's wife, yet He remained positive in the face of it all. He did not harbor bitterness. How he responded to this situation prepared him for bigger things to come. Job lost everything! His children, possessions, and he even became afflicted with sickness. His wife told him to curse God and die, yet Job decided to keep trusting God. In the end the Lord restored him giving him twice as much as he had, blessing His latter days more than His beginning.

A story is told of a man-Horatio Spafford, a successful lawyer and businessman. He lost his son to scarlet fever in 1871. The following year, there was a Chicago fire where he lost much of his business. He was a devout Christian who was an Elder in the Presbyterian Church and also volunteered at his friend's— D.L Moody— ministry. Two years after the Chicago fires, he decided to make a family trip to England knowing D.L

Moody was going to be preaching there that autumn. He was delayed due to a business dealing and so he sent his wife ahead with the four kids. A few days later, while crossing the Atlantic, their ship was struck by an iron sailing ship where several people lost their lives. All four of his daughters died leaving only his wife, who eventually made it to South Wales. While there she sent a telegram to her husband that said "Saved alone". He immediately embarked on a ship to meet his wife. When they got to the area where the other ship had sunk, the captain summoned him and showed him where the daughters had passed. The man returned to his cabin where it is said he wrote the words we so commonly sing today.

"When peace like a river, attendeth my way,
When sorrows like sea billows roll
whatever my lot, thou hast taught me to say
It is well, it is well, with my soul
It is well
With my soul
It is well, it is well with my soul."

In his deepest pain, he birthed a song that has outlived him and is still a blessing to many. In the face of challenges we must remain steadfast in God.

The way God designed us, He created in each of us that desire or longing for Him; however, He is not a dictator so He gives us choice. The deep desire is there and the only thing that can completely satisfy it is His

Word. Every other inconsequential thing we try to fill it up with is temporary. You get the thing and you are still searching. A big house, car, wealth, even in the face of challenges will still not bring you joy. Ask yourself why celebrities, who we think have it all, still end up committing suicide? The vacuum hasn't been filled with the right things and so there is a continuous longing.

Joshua 1:8

"Study this Book of Instruction continually. Meditate on it day and night so you will be sure to obey everything written in it. Only then will you prosper and succeed in all you do." NLT

Our prosperity and success in every area of life is therefore conditional on meditating on His Word. It's actually a guarantee. Stay close to the Word. We're told to love and serve the Lord our God with all our heart, our soul and all our mind. As you put these faculties into serving Him, it becomes a do or die affair. It's like your head isn't in the game anymore. Your mockers will unleash, especially when things seem to be delayed. Don't pay attention to them. Keep on serving God because He is a rewarder for those who diligently seek Him. He will not consume you without your consent, so sit at His feet, prepare the ground, and *allow* yourself to be consumed by Him. Once He consumes you, you become so lost in Him that you have no time to worry about anything else. Even when you make an effort to worry, you can't because you have entered a place of rest. Again, God doesn't write tragedies. If it's looking like one, then it definitely isn't the end yet. There's a purpose behind every challenge. You'll only see it if you exercise patience and look beyond it.

Isaiah 61:3: "*To console those who mourn in Zion, To give them beauty for ashes, The oil of joy for mourning, The garment of praise for the spirit of heaviness; That they may be called trees of righteousness, The planting of the LORD, that He may be glorified.*"

One day the Lord told me He could bring beauty out of ashes, and He began to explain to me how ashes come about. Then He said how we want the beauty but many don't want to go through the process that produces the ashes. It's a gruesome process, because you must go through the fire and get burnt in the process; however if we trust and depend on Him, the beauty of it shall come through. Don't lose hope as you trust God; you owe no explanation to anyone. There are people the enemy places on standby to discourage you in your faith walk, and you must recognize that. They'll make teasing statements and want you to explain your every move. I've heard too many negative things in the past so that I barely told anyone about my pregnancy with Josiah. I didn't want my faith tainted. I knew I was going to hear things like "What?" "Why?" "Again?" "Hasn't she learned from the past?" "Are you okay? Can you carry the pregnancy?" and so on. The only person I wanted to walk through this with was the Holy Spirit because I knew He understood me so well and I wanted us to win in the end.

A few days after Josiah's birth while I was still at the hospital, the Holy Spirit said to me, 'Many times, believers try hard to prove what God can do, or His existence. You don't have to prove My existence. I can prove Myself all by Myself." Therefore, it's okay to remain a fool in your servitude. The manifestation of your miracle will certainly silence the mockers. When that blessing comes stay in His presence. The Lord told me one day when I was about to give Josiah a bath: "It hurts my heart when my blessing keeps my people away from Me," so I vowed again to stay close to Him. As a believer , your top priority should be to seek the Kingdom of God, (Matthew 6:33), and when we do, the things we chase after will begin chasing us instead.

Don't throw in the towel. God is still on the throne. Some of you may be on your way to your promised land, keep pushing, keep pressing. Don't return to Egypt for the promised land is filled with milk and honey. Ask the Lord for patience as you wait on Him, otherwise you go seeking an Ishmael when He's prepared an Isaac for you. Remember the covenant was with Isaac, not Ishmael, so wait for yours so the covenant can be fulfilled. Ask for grace to go through your process, and push through those birth pangs, for on the other side of it, is an entire generation dependent on what's coming out of you. I heard an Apostle say "Your tears should not pain you. It should only reassure you, that if you cried, you will laugh." So though you may cry in the process, keep moving, because your season of laughter is coming.

In closing, let me say a short prayer for you:

Dear Lord, I thank you for your son/daughter. Thank You for all You've called them to be and what You're doing in their lives now. Thank You for the victories and thank You for the setbacks, because they're stepping stones to get to where You intend them to be. Father, I pray you strengthen them during these trying times. Give them hope. Comfort them. Wrap Your arms around them. Teach them Your ways as they wait on You. Every ungodly covenant entered into, on their behalf, I break it in the name of Jesus! You aren't a God of abandoned projects. I pray that what You've started in their lives, You bring into perfect completion. I release peace into that storm in Jesus' name. Amen!

Thank you for reading and I hope it was a blessing to you. Don't stop here. Please be a blessing to another who may be hurting. I leave you with another favorite verse of mine:

Psalms 46:1-3

"God is our refuge and strength, A very present help in trouble. Therefore we will not fear, Even though the earth be removed, And though the mountains be carried into the midst of the sea; Though its waters roar and be troubled, Though the mountains shake with its swelling."

No matter what you are going through, fear NOT. Any spirit— good or bad— that you give in to, or submit yourself to, controls your entire being. You become its puppet. It becomes your Master and takes control of you. It basically drives you. What happens to you in the physical is simply a manifestation of where you subjected yourself to that spirit in the spirit realm. It takes your body, soul and spirit to break yourself free from such.

Take the case of a victim of domestic abuse. She keeps the cycle going because she has already subjected herself to that dominant spirit of abuse; we keep asking ourselves why he or she keeps going back so many times.

A person under a false prophet has subjected themselves to that familiar spirit and so they act and do as that spirit inside of the false prophet tells them to do. Even if it looks foolish to you and I, they will keep on doing the foolishness.

The same applies to the spirit of fear. NEVER is it of God!! When you submit to it, it takes charge and controls you. You cower into it and become its puppet or slave. I break every spirit of fear that may have kept you bound in the Mighty Name of Jesus!

The Lord bless you and keep you!

RECOMMENDED/GOOD READS

(when facing challenging times)

- *From Wilderness to Wonders: Embracing the Power of Process* by Katherine Ruonala
- *Good Morning Holy Spirit* by Benny Hinn
- *What to Do When Faith Seems Weak and Victory Lost* by Kenneth E. Hagin
- *Hosting the Presence* by Bill Johnson
- *When Heaven Invades Earth* by Bill Johnson
- *Strengthen Yourself in the Lord* by Bill Johnson
- *Birthing the Miraculous* by Heidi Baker
- *The Spirit of Faith* by Mark Hankins
- *Dare to Believe* by Becky Dvorak
- *Supernatural Childbirth* by Jackie Mize

ABOUT THE AUTHOR

Carine Ndeh Njoh is a Doctor of Pharmacy (PharmD) who resides in Yukon, OK, with her family. She obtained her degree at Southwestern Oklahoma State University and relocated to Yukon upon her graduation. She has been through some very difficult trials in life that helped shape her into the person she is today. As a result, her desire is to help walk others through challenging times, so they recognize that God is ever present. She also developed an eminent passion for sharing the word of God with an emphasis on spiritual growth and intimacy with God. She is not a fan of religion, so she encourages Christians to freely worship the Father in spirit and truth, diving into deeper realms. She believes Christianity can be filled with faith and fun. Her hobbies include reading inspirational books and sharing laughter because laughter is good medicine!

Printed in Great Britain
by Amazon